Megachurches
& America's Cities

Megachurches
& America's Cities

How Churches Grow

John N. Vaughan

Baker Books

A Division of Baker Book House Co
Grand Rapids, Michigan 49516

Published by Baker Books
a division of Baker Book House Company
P.O. Box 6287, Grand Rapids, Michigan 49516-6287

Printed in the United States of America

Library of Congress Cataloging-in-Publication Data

Vaughan, John N.
  Megachurches and America's cities : how churches grow / John N.
  Vaughan.
    p. cm.
  Includes bibliographical references.
  ISBN 0–8010–9315–5
    1. Big churches. 2. City churches—North America—History—
20th century. 3. Church growth—North America—History—20th
century. 4. North America—Church history—20th history. I. Title.
  BV637.9.V375   1993
  250—dc20   93–7988

To
Dr. Jerry Falwell
Thomas Road Baptist Church
Lynchburg, Virginia

Contents

Acknowledgments

Without the cooperation of the statisticians of major denominations this compilation would have been impossible.

I am deeply grateful for their help.

Madonna Schweer, my secretary, diligently typed the manuscript. Special thanks also to: David Swisher, Diana Livingston, Kim Flippin, and Chris Stumph.

Thank you pastors, staff members, secretaries, and denominational leaders who for more than a decade have provided trust and information I have requested from you and your church. My prayer is that God will continue to perfect our relationship of mutual ministy for the strengthening of his churches and kingdom.

Introduction

As editor of the North American Society for Church Growth, director of the Church Growth and World Mission's center at Southwest Baptist University, and faculty member of the only university in the nation to offer a course exclusively on "Megachurches of the World," I have the opportunity to visit nearly two hundred churches annually. These congregations include the largest- and fastest-growing churches of the United States and the world. Some critics of large churches would ask me to apologize for this ministry God has so graciously provided. Gratitude, rather than apologizing for God, seems somehow more appropriate.

Much of the material in this text was presented as the Founder's Day Lecture for Liberty Baptist Theological Seminary, Lynchburg, Virginia.

Two photographs, one of Muslims and one of Christians, have dramatically impressed me during the past year. The picture of Christians is of six thousand people standing and facing the pulpit at the North Phoenix Baptist Church of Phoenix, Arizona. This church is the largest Southern Baptist Convention congregation in Sunday morning worship attendance, including children, in the western half of the United States. Dr. Richard Jackson, pastor of the church from 1967 to 1993, is a respected friend and faithful pastor. Worship attendance at the church increased from eight hundred people in 1960 to more than nine thousand in 1990. Under his leadership the church has baptized more than a thousand people annually since 1980.

As the church grows larger, and larger, and larger, the priority has always been introducing a world without Jesus Christ to the Savior. Growth of the congregation has been the natural result. Writing to his congregation in his weekly church newsletter article, Dr. Jackson shared:

> Our magnificent obsession at North Phoenix has been and always will be . . . soul-winning . . . New Testament evangelism . . . the making of disciples . . . the inducting or baptism of those disciples . . . and maturing of the saved. . . . This is not the decision of the pastor, nor is it the determination of some committee. . . . it is the unquestioned command of Our Lord Jesus Christ.[1]

North Phoenix Baptist Church reports more than two thousand trained soul-winners. According to church leaders, 95 percent of all persons baptized each year are new Christians who make a profession of faith to receive Jesus Christ as Lord and Savior.[2]

The second picture is an inside aerial view of nearly ten thousand Muslims at worship in an Indonesian mosque. A person would need to be numb spiritually to see the photo and remain unimpressed. Greg Bruckert, a Southern Baptist missionary, after completing his first term of mission service in Indonesia, was quoted in the denomination's foreign mission magazine, *The Commission,* as saying:

> In American churches, the "vision" is bigger and better mother churches, he has observed—let's build the super-church, let's get my church bigger. There are Southern Baptist churches in the States that are mission-minded, but I think there are a lot that want just to get bigger. And yet, in any culture, church-growth statistics say that the best way to reach people is not bigger churches—it's with new units. . . .[3]

As a member of the same denomination as the missionary, and as a faculty member teaching church growth in a Southern Baptist university, I absolutely agree with the need for churches, especially large churches, to be church planters. However, the brief quote from him in the magazine seems to become almost muted and overshadowed by the two page, color photograph mentioned above, on the pages immediately following his quote, showing the thousands of Muslims with faces bent toward the mosque floor and Mecca.

Large churches have been a continuing legacy throughout Christian history. Few new complaints can be offered by the critics. The "magnificent obsession" of the Great Commission still remains priority one for most large churches. Fairness surely demands that the large number of faithful churches not be judged and their motives questioned because of churches with less than biblical priorities.

My personal experience and contact with pastors of most of the largest churches in the United States and in other countries leads me to believe that many, I repeat many, of these men refuse to apologize for the growth God has given to their churches. Many of them make special efforts, however, not to do or say anything that might offend pastors and members of smaller congregations. American churches are filled with pastors and lay leaders with the Great Commission priority of Dr. Richard Jackson and the North Phoenix Baptist Church. Their growth records indicate that many of these churches aggressively and regularly create new units able to reach and mature new believers.

The following pages are intended to provide the most comprehensive and detailed update of the megachurch profile of North America. Readers interested in biblical and historical justification for large churches are directed to my earlier book *The Large Church*.[4] Specific topics discussed in that source include fourteen issues related to large churches (including authority, local autonomy, the carnality of competition, definitions of church, pastoral care, the potential for distorted doctrine), a selective history of large churches past and present, and images of the church (a search for definitions).

Increasingly, both small and large American churches are becoming more like third world megachurches. This likeness is demonstrating itself in the way United States congregations are moving toward multiple use of time, space, location, and staff for worship services. The issues actually have less to do with being a small or large church than with the problem-solving facing churches of all sizes. For example, as churches have grown larger, how are the common problems of limited space, limited staff, and the decision to meet at times other than eleven o'clock on Sunday morning addressed?

There is a subtle difference between a church merely filling its auditorium on Sunday morning and deciding to have multiple worship services and Sunday schools so that the biblical mandate to reach people can actually be fulfilled in this generation.

The historical problem has not been one of churches growing too large but rather the pathological tradition of filling a one hundred-seat auditorium, plateauing, and birthing additional churches through church splits. Typically, both ecclesiastical "birth control" and "abortion" have been the norm for churches of all sizes, rather than intentional expansion, extension, and bridging growth. The major issue facing both churches and classes within churches is the will and ability to reproduce existing groups and leadership. The frequent struggle between "small church" versus "large church" is actually an issue related to reproduction rather than one of size.

The most obvious examples of these pathological diseases can be found in most local congregations in the form of resistance to the suggestion of birthing new classes, making maximum use of building and parking space through multiple services before building new space, resistance to adding additional full- and part-time ministry staff, and increased focus of manpower, time, energy, and financial resources on the interests of church members to the exclusion of evangelism and missions.

To use the words of Dr. Othal Feather, former professor of Christian Education at Southwestern Baptist Theological Seminary, Fort Worth, Texas (the world's largest theological seminary), "When the compassion on the inside of the church exceeds the indifference of the world on the outside, the people will fill the churches." Growth, numerical and nurture, is the natural result of that compassion. These same results mandate planned use of the churches' finite resources of time, space, man power, and energies.

Churches that are willing to enlarge their use of these finite resources, as they invite the infinite resources of God, offer all of our churches valuable wisdom through both their successes and failures in learning to guide growth in healthy ways. Church leaders in all size churches do in fact make unfortunate mistakes in their search for right solutions. Any large church could write volumes on how not to grow a church, as it has, in the process of growing, discovered a few effective ways to cooperate with God in the growth of his churches. Tragically, many of the large church's critics tend to focus on the mistakes rather than the solutions that have allowed churches to grow larger as they reach, care for, and equip more and more people to become Great Commission people.

The time has come to cease the creation of false guilt and blame for growth that leads to larger churches. God will not be mocked and is fully capable of judging his own household. God will not apologize for the growth he provides for his churches and neither should we. If anything, we owe God our apologies for our unwillingness to cooperate with him in learning how to reach a lost and dying world.

The Megachurch Phenomenon

Until recent decades, any mention of large churches brought to mind images of the Cathedral of Notre Dame in Paris, Saint Peter's Basilica at the Vatican in Rome, Westminster Abbey in London, or Saint Paul's Cathedral in London. While several of these churches conduct multiple worship services, with the exception of Saint Peter's and its reported standing capacity of at least 40,000 people (some say 50,000), most of these cathedrals can accommodate only approximately 2,000 during each worship period. Mass at the largest service in Rome is reported to comprise nearly 8,000 worshipers.

After personal conversation with a representative of each church mentioned above, it was learned that Notre

Dame's estimated seating capacity is 1,850, with approximately 6,000 to 7,000 worshipers attending a combined six services. Their Saturday evening service averages 1,200 to 1,500 in attendance, while the earliest Sunday morning services may have 50 to 100 in attendance. Westminster Abbey has a capacity of 2,000, and total attendance for all five services averages 1,500 people. Saint Paul's Cathedral, with a seating capacity of 2,500, averages nearly 600 in the 10:30 A.M. service and approximately 400 in its 11:30 A.M. service for a total of 1,000 in attendance.

Historic cathedral-type churches in the United States include Washington, D.C.'s National Cathedral, New York City's Cathedral of Saint John the Divine, and Riverside Church. Saint John the Divine will average approximately 500 to 1,000 each week, while filling the sanctuary several times with a total of 12,000 for Christmas Eve. Riverside Church, located near Union Theological Seminary and Columbia University, fills its 2,500-seat sanctuary most weeks.

Megachurches: More Than Cathedrals

The rise of varied forms of megachurches is a phenomenon increasingly common to almost every continent. Recent interest is magnified by the growth of the 600,000–member Yoido Full Gospel Church, Seoul, Korea, from only 5 members in 1958. Still growing, as many as 10,000 new members each month in some years, in a city of more than 10 million people, the congregation has become the largest Christian congregation in the world today—and in Christian recorded history. As early as 1984, the congregation reported having 115 foreign missionaries ministering in sixteen different countries.

In his book *Answers to Your Questions*, Dr. David Yonggi Cho writes:

It doesn't matter whether a pastor has a big church or a small church. He must first form a foundation: a main goal of the church must be foreign outreach. From the beginning of any church, missions should be a priority.[1]

The Yoido church starts new daughter churches throughout Korea in five new locations each year. In past years the mother congregation is reported to have birthed at least three new congregations with 5,000 members each and another with 10,000 members. Imagine being able to begin a new church with 5,000 members on the first day of its ministry. Each year between 50,000 and 100,000 members are sent out by the congregation to establish new churches. More than a hundred new churches have been launched by the Yoido church, many much smaller than these just mentioned.

Similar accounts can be repeated for the growth of churches with attendance of 5,000 or more in Africa, China, Korea, South America, North America, Russia, and Australia. While more will be said later about the definition of the term "megachurch," the term is used by this writer to mean churches with at least an average weekly attendance of 2,000 or more people, including all children, in the primary worship service or services. In most cases, this attendance is on Sunday and occurs at several identical worship services ministering to totally different groups of people.

Not until research for the book *The World's 20 Largest Churches*[2] was it commonly known that the two largest Presbyterian churches, the two largest Methodist churches, and the largest Baptist congregation in the world are in Korea. However, even that research would have been difficult without prior research by C. Peter Wagner that had been published in *Look Out! The Pentecostals Are Coming*[3] and *Stop the World, I Want To Get On.*[4]

Cathedrals historically have been the official residence of major regional church officials within various state churches. A second function has been to serve as the regional or national corporate worship center for coronations, royal weddings, and national gatherings far exceeding the attendance capacities of the smaller parish churches that usually surrounded the cathedral. Finally, while cathedrals remain, to this day, the property of the denominations they represent, today's megachurches remain the sole vision and property of the local, and usually autonomous, congregation of people that brought about their construction.

Two significant books about megachurch growth in South America that provided some of the earliest information were William R. Read's *New Patterns of Church Growth in Brazil*[5] and Christian Lalive d'Epinay's *Haven of the Masses: A Study of the Pentecostal Movement in Chile.*[6] Many readers are unfamiliar with these important sources.

Most of the research concerning churches in the United States between 1967 and 1980 should be credited to Elmer L. Towns, who more than any other writer tracked large growing churches in Sunday school attendance and encouraged the growth of churches during the decade of the 1960s when both print and electronic media mounted a constant battle against the image of churches. After 1965, several mainline denominations were beginning to decline in Sunday worship attendance and membership.

Towns's article "The Ten Largest Sunday Schools," appearing in *Christian Life* magazine (September 1968) was soon followed by his best-selling book *The Ten Largest Sunday Schools and What Makes Them Grow.*[7] These and other publications by Towns during the 1970s revealed that growth in this nation was almost exclusively among Baptist congregations of both Southern and Independent Baptist varieties. Many American pastors and their people were encouraged by these accounts of large Sunday school attendance in churches such as Akron Baptist Temple (5,762), Highland Park Baptist Church of Chattanooga (4,821), First Baptist Church of Dallas (4,731), First Baptist Church of Hammond, Indiana (3,978), Canton Baptist Temple of

Canton, Ohio (3,581), Landmark Baptist Temple of Cincinnati (3,540), and others.[8]

By 1974 the modern large church movement was given continued exposure with Towns's book *The World's Largest Sunday School*,[9] the story of First Baptist Church of Hammond, Indiana. The church reported an average weekly Sunday school attendance of 7,837 in 1973. Lee Lebsack, that same year, wrote *Ten at the Top: How 10 of America's Largest Assemblies of God Grew.*[10] Eugene Skelton, a Southern Baptist employed by the Baptist Sunday School Board in Nashville, Tennessee, also wrote his book *10 Fastest Growing Southern Baptist Sunday Schools*[11] the same year.

The Billy Graham Evangelistic Association's publication division, World Wide Publications, shared the growth stories of fourteen large churches in *Decision* magazine and reprinted the articles in 1973 in book form. The book, *Great Churches of Today*,[12] included profiles of The People's Church (Toronto), Coral Ridge Presbyterian Church (Fort Lauderdale), Park Street Congregational Church (Boston), Garden Grove Community Church (now Crystal Cathedral Congregation of Garden Grove, California), Mount Zion Missionary Baptist Church (Los Angeles), Mount Olivet Lutheran Church (Minneapolis), and others.

Afro-American Churches: the Hidden Megachurches

Volumes have been written on the history of significant black pastors and their congregations that have had in the past, and continue today to have, dynamic and strategic roles in the mission of evangelizing America and the world.

Conspicuously absent from most listings of large and growing churches in past decades, however, were the large black congregations of the nation. Prior to the *Decision* magazine articles that included E. V. Hill's ministry at Mount Zion Missionary Baptist Church (Watts, Los Angeles) and *The Complete Book of Church Growth* by Elmer L. Towns,

John N. Vaughan, and David J. Seifert in 1981,[13] black churches were not included in other national listings of churches. As a contributor and as editor of that book, my major contributions were the inclusion of Concord Baptist Church (Brooklyn), Crenshaw Christian Center (Los Angeles), Evangel Temple (Washington, D.C.—a multiracial congregation), and others.

One reason for the omission referred to earlier had been the weakening in communication between black and white ethnic communities, especially after the disruptions following the Civil Rights and Black Power decades of the 1960s and 1970s. Thankfully, the willingness to share information between both communities of churches has increased since those dark days.

Among the most obvious omissions in previous decades was Dr. Adam Clayton Powell, Jr., who followed his father as pastor of the Abyssinian Baptist Church of New York City. Though it was the largest black Christian congregation in the nation (and probably in the world), only *Ebony* magazine and the secular press kept the public aware of the congregation. Powell is reported to have regularly preached to more than 4,000 people at the church and was pastor to more than 10,000 people by the age of twenty-three. As the only black member of the New York City Council and later as congressman from his state, he was constantly in the news.

The most recent, and most welcomed, contribution to literature about large black Christian churches has been written by Sid Smith, consultant in the Black Church Development Section of the Southern Baptist Sunday School Board. His book *10 Super Sunday Schools in the Black Community*[14] is the first book, to my knowledge, to cover fully several black churches in this decade. As a black Baptist, he has studied more than 300 black congregations in the past six years. All of the churches in his study are Baptist, with the exception of the Cathedral of Faith, Inkster, Michigan.

Some of the black churches he includes are Glendale Baptist Church (Miami), Emmanuel Baptist Church (San Jose), Mission of Faith Baptist Church (Chicago), Mount Zion Missionary Baptist Church (Los Angeles), and New Shiloh Baptist Church (Baltimore).

The independent nature of large congregations, both black and white, has made it difficult to gather reliable information in some instances. This same difficulty has also been experienced by some black denominational national offices that have sought to gather information about churches within their own national groups. However, information has been made increasingly available by churches willing to participate in the annual listing of the fastest-growing churches in *Church Growth Today* newsletter published by the author since 1986.[15]

Church Growth Today listed, in 1988–89, the Mount Ephraim Baptist Church of Atlanta, Georgia, as the fastest-growing church, the first black congregation, nationally, to be so listed. The Rev. R. L. White serves as pastor of this National Baptist Convention church. The newsletter reported:

> Mount Ephraim Baptist Church has the distinction of being the first black congregation to ever be listed as the fastest growing church in North America. They reported a growth [in Sunday morning average worship attendance—including all children], in multiple worship services, from 1,000 people in attendance in 1987 to 3,000 people in 1988 (a net gain of 2,000 different people in attendance). They reported an additional gain from the previous 3,000 in 1988 to an all-time record attendance of 4,000 in 1989.[16]

During that same twelve-month period from 1988 to 1989, eight of the twelve fastest-growing churches in the nation were black congregations. The six affiliation groups represented among the eight churches included: Independent Charismatic (INDC), Church of God in Christ

(COGIC), African Methodist Episcopal Church (AME), United Methodist Church (UMC), National Baptist Convention (NBC), and National Baptist Convention of America (NBCA). Again, the next year, 1989–1990, the three fastest-growing churches in the nation were black congregations. The fastest-growing congregation was World Changers, led by pastor Creflo Dollar, in College Park, Georgia, a suburb south of Atlanta's airport. The congregation grew in average worship attendance from 1,500 to 4,800 people.[17]

Megachurches of the Past

Church buildings designed to accommodate several thousand people were commonly reported as early as AD 323. The grand cathedral built by Constantine in Constantinople is reported to have covered an area of 55,000 square feet, was built by 10,000 workmen under the direction of 100 foremen, and had a staff fixed by Justinian at 60 pastors, 100 deacons, 40 deaconesses, 90 subdeacons, 100 readers, 25 singers, and 100 custodians/porters. Since churches did not have pews until about AD 1100, approximately 10,000–20,000 people could have attended any one public worship service (assuming that there was only one gathering each Sunday). This reference from Thomas F. Mathews's *The Early Churches of Constantinople: Architecture and Liturgy*[18] is also further discussed in *The Large Church*.[19]

The era of great cathedral building flourished from the eleventh through the sixteenth centuries in France, Germany, England, Italy, Spain, and Latin America. Later, in March 1861, Charles Spurgeon's 25,225-square-foot Metropolitan Tabernacle, seating 6,000 people, was dedicated in London. He preached to more than 5,000 each week.

Meanwhile, in the United States, Charles Finney was preaching to 2,000–3,000 at Chatham Street Chapel in New York City. The African Methodist Church in Charleston,

South Carolina, grew from 1,000 to 3,000 members. Henry Ward Beecher regularly addressed 2,000 people at Brooklyn's Plymouth Church. The black pastor John Jasper, beginning with only 9 members, led First African Baptist Church of Richmond, Virginia, to a weekly attendance of as many as 2,000 people.[20]

As early as 1891, Wilbur Chapman pastored "the world's largest Protestant church" at Bethany Presbyterian Church in Philadelphia. The church's seating capacity is reported to have been 4,820, with regular attendance averaging 3,000–5,000. DeWitt Talmage, in 1874, led Brooklyn Tabernacle to build a 5,000-seat auditorium, which was rebuilt to seat 6,000 after a fire in 1889. L. K. Williams, pastor of the Olivet Baptist Church, Chicago, reached a total of 8,743 members, with 3,100 in Sunday school. According to Carter G. Woodson in *The History of the Black Church*, this large black church reported forty-two departments and auxiliaries with 512 officers, of whom 24 were paid workers.[21]

In 1916 P. H. Welshimer led First Christian Church of Canton, Ohio, to grow far beyond most churches of his era and region. The church reached 7,009 attendees for Sunday school, while First Christian Church of Columbus, Ohio, reported an attendance of 7,147 people on the final Sunday of a fifteen week attendance campaign. Francis M. Arant, biographer of Welshimer, concluded, "The average for the fifteen weeks was: Columbus 3,117, and Canton 3,033."[22]

Aimee Semple McPherson led Angelus Temple, a Foursquare Gospel church in Los Angeles, to fill its 5,400 seat auditorium. By 1922 she was conducting thirty-two healing services in the building each week. Other sources and details are available in the book *The Large Church*.[23]

While planning future issues of *Church Growth Today* newsletter, it occurred to the editor to examine what a list of the world's largest congregations would have looked like more than twenty-five years ago during the decade of the mid-1960s. The information summarized in table 1 was based on available resources and some personal research.

Table 1 World's Largest Churches during the Mid-1960s		
Members *Congregation*		*Pastor*
1. 40,000	Jotabeche Methodist Pentecostal Santiago, Chile	Javier Vasquez
2. 17,000	Akron Baptist Temple Akron, Ohio	Dallas Billington
3. 14,000	First Baptist Church Dallas, Texas	W. A. Criswell
4. 11,400	Young Nak Presbyterian Church Seoul, Korea	Han, Kyung Chik
5. 10,000	Abyssinian Baptist Church New York, New York	Adam Clayton Powell, Jr.
6. 9,000	Bellevue Baptist Church Memphis, Tennessee	Ramsey Pollard
7. 5,800	First Baptist Church Hammond, Indiana	Jack Hyles
8. 5,000	Yoido Full Gospel Church Seoul, Korea	David Yonggi Cho

Source: John N. Vaughan, "The Megachurch Phenomenon," *Church Growth Today*, vol. 1, no. 4, April 1986, 3.

Radical changes for growing churches of the United States and the world have occurred since the decade of the sixties. Since that time the definition of a large church has come to include ever-larger congregations. Louis Entzminger's 1949 listing of the largest American churches in *How to Organize and Administer a Great Sunday School*[24] included First Baptist Church of Fort Worth, Texas. The church averaged 5,200 people in Sunday school attendance at that time. By 1990 the highest average weekly Sunday school attendance was 20,000—at First Baptist Church of Hammond, Indiana.

Information in the following tables quite dramatically illustrates the church growth of recent decades. Table 2 shows the Sunday school attendance range of the ten largest churches for four different decades. Table 3 gives more recent worship attendance figures. The reader should be aware that worship attendance currently exceeds Sunday school attendance in most churches. A comparison of range-in-worship attendance among the world's ten largest churches follows, in table 4.

Table 2 Sunday school Attendance Range Among
the 10 Largest U.S. Churches, 1949–1990

Year	High Attendance	Low Attendance
1949	5,200	552
1969	5,762	2,453
1979	15,101	4,348
1990	20,000*	5,210

Sources: 1949, Louis Entzminger, *How to Organize and Administer a Great Sunday School* (Fort Worth: The Manney/Company, 1949), iii; *1969*, Elmer L. Towns, *The Ten Largest Sunday Schools and What Makes Them Grow* (Grand Rapids: Baker, 1969), 154–63; *1979*, Elmer L. Towns, John N. Vaughan, and David J. Seifert, *The Complete Book of Church Growth* (Wheaton: Tyndale, 1981), 356; *1990*, John N. Vaughan.

*Verified in correspondence with Jack Hyles, senior pastor of First Baptist Church, Hammond, Indiana, 1993.

Table 3 Worship Attendance Range Among
the 10 Largest U.S. Churches, 1980 and 1990

Year	High Attendance	Low Attendance
1980	13,000	4,700
1990	20,000	8,000

Sources: 1980, Elmer L. Towns, John N. Vaughan, and David J Seifert, *The Complete Book of Church Growth* (Wheaton: Tyndale, 1981), 349–50; *1990,* John N. Vaughan.

Table 4 Worship Attendance Range Among
the 10 Largest World Churches, 1982 and 1990

Year	High Attendance	Low Attendance
1982	105,000	9,960
1990	320,000*	42,000

Source: John N. Vaughan

*Founded in 1958 with only five people, the Yoido Full Gospel Church of Seoul, Korea, reported an average Sunday worship attendance (includes all children) of 320,000 for the year 1990 at the main campus of the congregation and an additional 280,000 people at the church's satellite chapels. Pastor of the church is Dr. David Yonggi Cho.

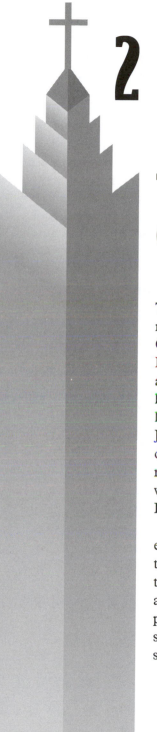

The Language of Growth

The early months of 1981 will be remembered by some as violent times. On Tuesday, March 30, President Ronald Reagan was shot in the chest after speaking to a Washington, D.C., labor convention. Forty-four days later, on Wednesday May 13, Pope John Paul II was shot twice in the abdomen by an escaped Turkish criminal while surrounded by ten thousand worshipers in Saint Peter's Square. Both leaders lived.

Meanwhile, between these two events, a small group of forty Christians met in West Haven, Connecticut, to organize a new church. West Haven, a small city of nearly fifty thousand population, located only five miles south of New Haven and Yale University, has witnessed amazing growth of that church. Just one decade later, Richard Mallette leads the one thousand people who attend Living Word Ministries, an Independent Charismatic congregation.

Ten years earlier a gathering of 157 believers met in the northeastern Atlanta suburb of Stone Mountain, Georgia, to organize the Smoke Rise Baptist Church. By 1980, the year before the Connecticut group began its ministry, this Southern Baptist congregation reported an average attendance of 700 Sunday morning worshipers. People continued to invite friends and during the one-year period of 1989 to 1990 attendance increased by 300 new attenders. Since that first worship service nearly two decades ago, the church has increased by an average number of people equal to those original 157 organizers every two years. Led by Pastor J. Truett Gannon, weekly attendance is growing from 1,800 toward 4,000 people.

Taped messages that tell the dramatic story of the growth of the Saddleback Valley Community Church of Mission Viejo, California, have been ordered by thousands of pastors and church leaders from at least forty-nine countries. Pastor Rick Warren has taught pastors and church leaders from more than sixty denominations the principles he has learned regarding how to and how not to grow a church. Located in the Saddleback Valley, a cluster of planned communities about one hour south of Los Angeles International Airport, this church has grown from one family to 4,400 people in weekly attendance during its first eleven years. The church has experienced continued growth while also starting sixteen daughter churches. Recently the Southern Baptist congregation was listed in *Church Growth Today* newsletter as the fourth fastest-growing church in the United States.

The cover of the July/August 1988 issue of *MissionsUSA* magazine printed the captivating caption, "Rick Warren: Zero to 4,000 in Eight Years." Sherri Brown, in her cover article, wrote:

As a Southwestern Baptist Theological Seminary (Ft. Worth, Texas) student, he combed the library for every book on church growth. He found 72. He read them all. He developed a questionnaire and sent it to the 100 largest churches in the United States.

As graduation approached, he and his wife poured over maps trying to determine where God wanted them to plant a church . . . .

Eventually they settled on Orange County, California, the fastest growing county in the United States from 1970 to 1980. "I knew there would be enough people there to challenge me for the rest of my life," says Warren. "The challenge would always be bigger than the church."

In January 1980, Warren and his wife, with their 4-month-old daughter, Amy, packed their belongings in a U-Haul trailer and headed for California. Not knowing anyone, they pulled into a real estate office where they met Don Dale. "I'm here to start a church," Warren said. "I need a place to live and I have no money."[1]

The rest of the Saddleback story is rapidly becoming history. Today the pastor reports that 70 percent of those who attend become Christians through the ministry of the congregation. Rick shares with other church leaders, "We exist for the unbeliever!" The congregation met in a Mission Viejo high school until 1993 when it bought land for the construction of a new worship and ministry center. Since early 1993 it has conducted worship services in a tent capable of seating several thousand people. During the church's first decade its people have met in more than fifty different meeting places. The church relocated to a new property in December, 1992, and attendance increased from 6,000 to a new level of 8,000 people by early 1993.

Today, the Willow Creek Community Church, located in the northwest Chicago suburb of South Barrington, Illinois, ranks with First Baptist Church of Hammond, Indiana, as one of the two largest churches in the United States in week-by-week attendance. Started by Bill Hybels and a small group of committed friends in 1975, while Hybels was a student at Trinity College in Deerfield, Illinois, the church took its name from the Willow Creek Theater in Palentine, Illinois, where it first met for worship. During those early years the pastor and youth sold tomatoes door-to-door to raise additional money for church project expenses.

While the Saddleback Church reaches out to "Saddleback Sam" with the Gospel, the Willow Creek Church focuses on the needs of "Unchurched Harry." As friends invited friends and strangers, attendance grew an additional 1,374 people from 1988–89 and was ranked in *Church Growth Today* as the third fastest-growing church in the nation.[2] Now, only sixteen years after it was started, an average of more than 15,000 people attend the Saturday evening and Sunday morning services.

Dr. David Yonggi Cho began the Yoido Full Gospel Church of Seoul, Korea, as a small tent church with only five people on May 8, 1958, and it has become the most researched congregation on earth. The church reported the average 1991 worship attendance in its seven services as being 320,000 people on their main campus and 280,000 people attending satellite chapels. The congregation has become both the world's largest church and the largest church in recorded Christian history. There have been years when this church has increased in membership by more than 10,000 people.

Since the founding of Asia's first twentieth-century megachurch, the Young Nak Presbyterian Church of Seoul, by Dr. Kynung Chik Han and his band of 27 members in 1945, many Korean churches have experienced growth unique in Christian history. In 1984, it was announced in the book *The World's 20 Largest Churches* that for the first time, the largest Assembly of God, Baptist, Presbyterian, and Methodist congregations in the world were in Korea.

The story of these six churches is not one of isolated growth. Each one represents many growth miracles unknown to most churches and most Christians. Their doctrine and methods may differ, but their priority of sharing the good news of Jesus Christ remains immovable. They represent the churches able to experience growth to the 1,000, 2,000, 4,000, and beyond-10,000 levels in average weekly attendance.

Before much more is said about definitions of terms, a brief word about three contemporary contributors of information and views about large churches in the United States needs mention. Though more could be said about my friend and mentor Elmer L. Towns, now dean of Liberty Baptist Seminary in Lynchburg, Virginia, I will narrow my attention to Lyle E. Schaller, Carl F. George, and Peter Drucker. Each of these men is becoming increasingly involved in the larger church arena. These three men are mentioned to identify the significance of the present book from their three perspectives. You as a reader are encouraged to become thoroughly knowledgeable about books written by all three men, in addition to the many books by Towns.

Lyle E. Schaller

Most pastors and church-growth readers know the articles and books of Lyle E. Schaller. He is most readily identified for his extensive leadership as a church planner, as a consultant for more than thirty years, and serving as editor of the *Creative Leadership Series* for Abingdon Press.

Among his more than thirty-five books are his earlier works *Planning for Protestantism in Urban America* (1965), *The Local Church Looks to the Future* (1968), and *The Change Agent* (1972). In his 1975 book, *Hey, That's Our Church!*, he indicated that churches with an average weekly worship attendance of 350 and more were in the top 95th percentile of the approximately 500,000 churches in the nation. During the 1980s three of his books focused increasingly on larger churches. His trilogy of special interest to us includes *The Multiple Staff and the Large Church* (1980), *The Middle Sized Church* (1985), and *The Senior Minister* (1988).

The Multiple Staff and the Large Church identified the church of 700 or larger in worship attendance as a "mini-denomination." That classification was the term used for the largest category of congregation. Worship attendance is mentioned more frequently in this book than in many of his previous books.

Schaller's most recent book is *The Seven Day a Week Church* (1992). The terms of choice for the book tend to be "full-service church" and "very large church."

Carl F. George

As director of the Charles E. Fuller Institute of Evangelism and Church Growth, Pasadena, California, Carl F. George is well-known as a church-growth consultant. He is coauthor of *Leading and Managing Your Church* with Robert E. Logan (1987) and is author of *Prepare Your Church for the Future* (1991). The first written reference to the term *metachurch* currently being used by Carl George is by C. Peter Wagner in the *Dictionary of Pentecostal and Charismatic Movements* (1988). Wagner mentions Carl George and refers to "megachurch (several thousands of members) to the metachurch (several tens of thousands)."[3] The term "metachurch," then, was defined as a church of "several tens of thousands" of members.

Carl George, when referring in his 1991 book to Paul Heibert, originator of the term *metachurch*, makes passing reference to church size,[4] but majors on the dynamics involved in growth. In his book *Prepare Your Church for the Future*, he states:

The name Meta-Church, then, is quite distinct from megachurch. This new label allows for greater numbers, but its deepest focus is on change: pastors' changing their minds about how ministry is to be done. . . . A Meta-Church could be, as it grows, the size of a large church, superchurch or megachurch. But because its potential scale of operation so far exceeds these other classes of churches, it should have its own name, whatever its size.[5]

This statement, when compared with the statement accompanying the chart of church sizes[6] that goes from "super church" (1,000–3,000) to "mega church" (3,000–10,000) to "meta church" (10,000+), suggests that what we are in fact discussing is a "Type A" megachurch (3,000–10,000) and a "Type B" megachurch (10,000+). See page 50ff for a full description of these terms.

His use of the phrase, "potential scale," sounds innocent enough, but American churches have a terrible record of borrowing ideas without dismantling them—especially home cell groups. His statement, that "the North American megachurch seems to have stalled"[7] is unfounded. During 1988–89, a total of fifty-three churches in the United States broke the next 1,000-barrier mark in worship attendance. For example, eighteen churches previously in the 1,000-attendance range moved up and broke the 2,000-attendance barrier. Results from research at Southwest Baptist University, shown on table 5, illustrate the commonly untold story of churches—all size churches, but especially megachurches—that are breaking previous attendance barriers for the first time. An average of ten congregations in the United States report a net gain of 1,000 or more in worship attendance each year. During the year 1989–90, a record number of twenty United States churches increased by 1,000 or more in worship attendance.

The major categories of barrier-breaking churches are Southern Baptist and Assemblies of God churches growing through the multiplication of Sunday school groups, according to data here at the Church Growth and World Missions Center. These two denominational bodies also consistently have the largest number of existing and newly emerging megachurches in the United States.

Regrettably, Carl George seems to have a low view of Sunday school churches and fails to recognize that both United States and Korean megachurches/metachurches represent less than one-tenth of one percent of all churches in each of our nations. Only seventeen of Korea's nearly thirty thousand churches report 10,000 or more in worship attendance in 1990. This figure includes children, which are usually not included in Korean statistics. They are, however, included by the Church Growth and World Missions Center at Southwest Baptist University in Missouri. The United States currently has six churches reporting an average weekly attendance of 10,000 or more people. America's fastest growing churches demonstrate that Sunday school groups continue to be the premier small-growth-group model in the nation.

Less than 1 percent of the home group churches in the United States have groups that are either by philosophy of ministry or organizational structure designed to multiply in the manner both Carl George and I know to be needed. This is fact, not theory, since my office gathered the 1990 church census data from the Independent churches of the United States. We know more about Independent churches than they know about themselves, when it comes to a national picture of small-group health and pathology. I welcome Carl George to the megachurch/metachurch ranks but not at the expense of minimizing the metachurch structure of choice in North America. This in no way minimizes the churches that each of us works with that do not have Sunday school groups and request our help in starting home cell groups. Metachurch dynamics include Sunday school group multiplication rather than exclude them.

Table 5 Barrier-Breaking U.S. Megachurches in Average Weekly Worship Attendance During the 12-Month Period 1988–89

Number of Churches	Barrier Broken
18	2,000
14	3,000
10	4,000
6	5,000
1	6,000
1	7,000
1	8,000
1	9,000
1	12,000

Source: John N. Vaughan
Note: A total of 53 U.S. churches broke the indicated worship-attendance barrier for the first time during the above 12-month period.

As one who has personally visited the twenty largest churches of Korea, has taught on the subject of home cell groups in Korea, and as one who knows several of the pastors of Korea's largest churches, I know that Korea probably has about the same percentage of nongrowing churches as we have in the United States. Many Korean churches have nongrowing home cell groups, just as we in America have many churches with nongrowing Sunday schools . . . and home cell groups.

The problem is not only with the proper purpose and design of Sunday school or home cell groups, by whatever name we call them, but rather in their proper use in our churches. Churches split and fail to grow in Korea just as in the United States. As compiler of the first list of United States and world home cell group churches and the only published listing of the largest churches in the United States and the world, I do not speak as a novice. This word of caution, if ignored, is to the possible peril of continued kingdom effectiveness in North America beyond A.D. 2000. Home group pastors of many of the largest ministries in America know that my caution has merit.

If the term "metachurch" continues to carry with it a low view of Sunday school as a viable metachurch group while substituting home groups almost exclusively at this period in our history, this narrow privatization of the term *metachurch* cannot justly or seriously go unchallenged. Both groups represent the highest domain of numerical growth of the largest churches in both Korea and America. Such growth, however, for most churches of the world, is relegated to the domain of church-growth theory rather than perceived reality.

Peter F. Drucker

Peter F. Drucker is a treasure to the church. His emerging interest in the effectiveness of churches will without question benefit all of us. His support of the author's role in megachurch research is greatly appreciated.

To the reader unfamiliar with him, we recommend his classic book, *Management,* as an introduction. He is known to millions in American business and economic circles as the preeminent business and management writer of our time. Two of his most recent books are *Managing the Non-Profit Organization* (1990) and *Managing for the Future* (1992).

As the role of today's megachurches in reaching America's cities is being considered, however, the reader should particularly be aware of one quote from his book *The New Realities* and a second from *Managing for the Future.*

> Around 1970 there were no more than five thousand pastoral churches with a membership of two thousand parishioners or more. By the late eighties their number had grown fourfold, to twenty thousand. And they alone employ probably more than a million volunteers as unpaid staff.[8]

Fifteen years ago there were few such churches around, and most were quite small. Today there are some 20,000 large pastoral churches, each with a membership of 2,000 people or more—and some 5,000 of them have congregations in excess of 4,000 or 5,000.[9]

There is reason to seriously question Drucker's reference of 20,000 U.S. churches with memberships of 2,000 or more people. Large churches in the United States are much easier to locate than smaller churches. There are simply more of the smaller churches. The largest clearing house for lists of churches in the nation is American Church Lists, Inc., of Arlington, Texas. This list house reports having the addresses of 355,232 United States congregations, Christian and non-Christian, in its files. Church membership size is available for 147,513 churches (or 41.5% of the total). This source also lists 3,357 churches with a reported total membership of 1,800 or more people.

Since the figure of 147,513 churches represents only 41.5 percent of their total list of churches, and assuming that there was at least an equal percentage of 1,800-plus member churches in the remaining "membership unknown" churches, there would be a possibility of approximately 8,084 churches with 1,800 or more members. This assumes, however, that large churches are more difficult to find or to get membership information from than the storefront church that either has no telephone or a hard-to-reach bi-vocational pastor.

Let's go one additional step. Assume that there are at least 500,000 churches in the nation rather than the statistical "universe" of 355,232 churches in the list house's files. If there are an estimated 8,084 churches of at least 1,800 members among the smaller universe of 355,232 churches, then in a larger universe of 500,000 churches, there could be an estimated 11,378 churches that same size. This very optimistic estimate would still be only 56 percent of Drucker's 20,000 churches with a membership of 2,000 or more members. By lowering the membership size to 1,800 members or more, we have added an additional benefit to the 20,000 estimation. If only churches of 2,000 members and larger were considered, we would have fewer than the 11,378 churches this size in the larger universe of churches.

This becomes vital to any strategy for reaching America's cities, because it allows us to know the size of the army available to us as an evangelistic team of congregations nationally. To overestimate our resources could prove to be unnecessarily costly to us. In no way is this to suggest that God cannot or will not use our little and make much of it as described many times in the Bible.

A New United States Megachurch Every Two Weeks

Large churches have always been part of Christian history. The reader interested in additional detail of the history of large churches will be interested in chapter 1, "The Limits of Growth," in *The World's 20 Largest Churches*[10] and chapter 2, "A Selective History of Large Churches, Past and Present," in *The Large Church*.[11]

Large churches are part of our history. The recent rise of larger and larger churches at an increasingly faster rate of growth is unique to this final quarter of the twentieth century. While monarchs and wealthy benefactors have led in the construction of cathedrals during past centuries, the present willful, and even joyful, erection of very large church buildings as worship centers for thousands and tens of thousands of worshipers, by common men, is unique in Christian history.

The largest congregations in Christian history are being built today. "Congregation" should be understood as a local network of baptized believers committed to Jesus Christ and one another for the Great Commission purposes of both

Christian nurture and worldwide evangelism. Further, the term implies personal and corporate maturity in Christian attitudes and skills that reflect the living presence and power of Jesus Christ.

More is meant than a mere gathering of people, a crowd, as at a concert or athletic event, where only passive attention may be required or desired. Worldwide there are more than forty churches with a weekly attendance of at least 10,000 people. The first published listing of the world's fifty largest churches was provided by this writer for *The Almanac of the Christian World: 1991–1992.*[12]

In the United States a new congregation breaks the 2,000-worship attendance barrier nearly every two weeks. This average weekly attendance is not just the attainment of a high turnout for some isolated special event. These congregations are attaining this average attendance for a period of at least one full year and in most cases for the first time in the congregation's history.

The Megaministry Principle

The terminology used to describe the recent surge of increased growth in churches is undergoing transition. The first distinction that needs to be made before the new language of large growth can be discussed is the difference between a "megaministry" and a "megachurch."

A congregation with an average Sunday morning worship attendance of a hundred people each week might be considered by many to be a small church. However, this size church would be considered a large church by most churches of the world that average less than that number.

A church located nearly ten miles from our university campus has an average Sunday morning worship attendance of nearly 100 people each week. When you realize that the small town where the church is located has a total population of only 300 people, it becomes obvious that the church has a significant and even far-reaching ministry.

Few churches can claim to be reaching one-third of their town or city in attendance each week. Very few churches with several thousand people attending weekly can claim to have saturated their city as well as this church in a town of 300 people. The Thomas Road Baptist Church located in Lynchburg, Virginia, reports an average weekly Sunday morning worship attendance of 11,000 people. In their 1971 book, *Church Aflame*, Jerry Falwell and Elmer Towns wrote in the final two pages of the last chapter, "The City and the Future of the Church":

> Lynchburg, Virginia, is a small town of 53,000 population located in the heart of the state. One would think the town is too small to provide the setting for a large church, yet nearly 20% of the town's population are members of the Thomas Road Baptist Church.[13]

These two churches, one small and another very large, both illustrate the principle I call the "megaministry principle." The size of the church in relation to its city or ministry area is the significant factor rather than church size alone. A congregation of any size can be a megaministry church. Pastors and churches make a great mistake in minimizing the size of a city or of a church without viewing the potential the church has for saturating its geographical ministry area with the gospel. Falwell and Towns, in chapter 7 of the same book, comment:

> Saturation is preaching the gospel to every available person at every available time by every available means. The concept of saturation is scripturally reflected in Acts 5:28 where the church leaders in Jerusalem were accused: "Ye have filled Jerusalem with your doctrine." Falwell states plainly that his intention is to fill all Lynchburg with the doctrine of the Scriptures. The method by which the early

church disciples accomplished the saturation of Jerusalem is, "Daily in the temple and in every house they ceased not to teach and preach Jesus Christ" (Acts 5:42). Later Paul reaffirms this method of saturation, "And have taught you publicly and from house to house" (Acts 20:20). "I cease not to warn every one night and day with tears" (Acts 20:31).[14]

Principle: The megaministry principle addresses the issue of proportion rather than size alone. It is the conviction of this writer that any and all Bible-centered and teaching ministries, whatever their size, are eternally significant to God and his kingdom.

Several categories of megaministries are listed below to insure a clearer understanding of terms.

Class A Megaministries

"Class A" megaministries are congregations currently having *20 percent of the city or county's population* actively involved in either membership or regular weekly attendance. These churches are usually located in towns or cities with less than 70,000 in population.

Class B Megaministries

"Class B" megaministries by definition include any churches having a *regular attendance that exceeds membership or adherents*. Saturation is the method at the heart of this principle and can be illustrated by both small and large churches. By this definition a large church in an even larger city may have a large ministry when compared to much smaller churches but in actuality may or may not have a megaministry.

Class C Megaministries

"Class C" megaministries are churches considered as *large within the context of their own denominational definitions of "large."* Small denominations tend to produce smaller "large" congregations than larger denominations. Class C megaministries are measured by size within their own denomination or affiliation groups rather than by local-ministry area, county or metropolitan area, immediately surrounding the church.

For example, national data reported in the 1989 General Minutes of the United Methodist Church indicated that nearly 4 percent (3.5%) of all their congregations have an average weekly worship attendance of 350 or more people. However, this percentage represents approximately 20 percent, or one person in every five, of the average weekly worship attendance of 3,421,642 people in United Methodist churches.

Larger-attendance United Methodist churches, reporting 500 or more attendees each Sunday, represent only about 2 percent (1.5%) of all churches within the denomination. However, this seemingly small percentage of churches constitute approximately 10 percent of all people worshiping in the major service of United Methodist churches each Sunday. These same percentages vary from denomination to denomination in comparisons of their own total national worship attendance with that of their churches reporting at least 350 people.

Class D Megaministries

"Class D" megaministries are measured by the rate of growth the congregation is experiencing during a defined period of time. Class D *churches are churches experiencing an annual average weekly worship attendance net gain of at least 100 or more people.* Churches in this category are usually, but not always, where the emerging megachurches can be found. These churches receive special attention and study at the Church Growth and World Missions Center and Megachurch Research Press directed by this writer.

Most churches have a "front door" and/or "side doors" through which new members enter and become active members. All churches also have a "back door" through which members exit as they leave the congregation because of job transfers, preference for another congregation, conflict, or death.

C. Peter Wagner, in *Leading Your Church to Growth,* provides practical guidelines for measuring the size of a church's back door.

> Other churches are growing by standing still. Churches which have a primary ministry in a community of extremely high mobility such as a college town or near a military base do not grow easily. It is not uncommon for such churches to see an annual attrition rate of 30 percent or more. This compares to a national average of around 7 percent. Many of these churches have excellent outreach programs; they are leading large numbers of unbelievers to Jesus Christ and folding them into the church, but year after year the church just stays about the same.[15]

For a congregation to grow numerically beyond the previous year, there must first be a replacement of members lost through the back door. Only when this replacement has been accomplished can a church have net growth and existing empty seats filled with new people who will hear the good news of Jesus Christ.

Annual research information reported in *Church Growth Today* newsletter indicates that an estimated 400 to 650 congregations among the more than 500,000 United States churches have a net growth of 100 or more people each year. This listing of Sunday morning worship attendance also includes all children on the church property, counting all people and groups only once.

Worship attendance is used as the measure, rather than Sunday school attendance, because many ethnic and non-denominational congregations usually report either small or no Sunday schools for participants above the twelfth grade. This explanation is important since Sunday school churches tend to be far more effective at assimilating visitors and new members than churches with other types of small groups.

Even with only 400–650 congregations reporting an average weekly worship attendance gain of 100 or more annually, all size congregations are always represented among Class D megaministries.

Congregations showing the greatest ability for growth of this magnitude tend to have an average attendance of 200–299, 400–599, 1000–1999, or 2000–2999.

Class E Megaministries

"Class E" megaministries are congregations with an *average weekly worship attendance of at least 350–1,000 people.* While these congregations tend to average only about 5 percent, the congregations reporting 350 or more in worship attendance, they average a calculated 20 percent of the congregations within many denominations (see table 6).

Table 6 Approximate Percentage of Average National
Worship Attendance Each Week
for 350-Plus-Attendance Churches
(Selected Denominations)

Affiliation	Churches with 350+ Worship	% of Total Churches	% of Total Attendance
Church of God (Anderson, Ind.)	48	2	14
Church of Nazarene	136	3	1

Churches of Christ	425	3	19
Disciples	57	2	6
Evangelical Free Church	103	10	40
Lutheran (ELCA)	755	7	1
Presbyterian (PCA)	70	7	37
Presbyterian (PCUSA)	570	5	27
Southern Baptist	2298	6	30
United Methodist	1280	4	20
Total	5742	(average) 5	(average) 20

Note: These 10 affiliation groups represent a total aggregate of 123,608 congregations. Data from current denominational yearbooks. ©1993 by John N. Vaughan

The Megachurch Principle

Principle: Once a congregation has broken the proverbial "200 barrier" of worship attendance, great growth tends to occur as space, groups, resources, and staff are doubled with planned regularity.

Research results gathered from rapid-growing churches at the Church Growth and World Research Missions Center clearly demonstrates that this is perhaps the most vital of all organizational principles common to large churches that are experiencing considerable growth. The decision to multiply group sanctuary, educational (especially preschool and children), and/or parking space as worship attendance nears 80 percent saturation allows the church the unique opportunity to tilt attendance toward continued growth.

Table 7 Large Church Summary: 350+ Worship Attendance, 1990

AFF	Total Churches	350–499	500–599	600–699	700–799	800–899	900–999	1000–1999	2000–2999	3000–3999	4000–4999	5000–5999	6000–6999	7000–7999	8000–8999	9000–9999	10,000
AG	11,536	324	112	68	47	46	19	89	19	3	4	2					1
BBF	3,025	189	32	18	9	12	7	28		1	1	1					
CC	13,174	302	83	45	25	17	15	35	4	4	1						
COGA	2,336	26	8	5	2	3		4	2								
DIS	9,078	51	7	5		4	1	2	1								
EFC	1,046	49	15	14	10	5	2	8	1				1				
ELCA	11,507	493	103	74	33	28	10	23	4			1					
L-MO	6,031	314	110	58	52	21	16	25	4	2							
NAZ	5,172	76	21	11	9	6	3	9	1								
PCA	1,055	28	13	10	3	4	3	14	2		1						
PCUSA	11,501	258	77	40	21	21	8	34	2	2	1						
SBC	38,221	1,140	336	214	154	107	71	221	36	10	5		2	1		1	
UCC	6,338	96	21	5	3	2	2	1	1								
UMC	36,698	735	222	104	43	44	27	47	7	2							

Source: John N. Vaughan and staticians of groups listed above. © Copyright 1993.

3

The Barrier-Breaking Decade

Most churches decide to terminate numerical growth once their space nears saturation. Growth is often viewed as satisfactory when a church has enough people to fill the vacant seats and ministries left behind by members who leave the church. Churches with momentum for continued growth often hesitate because of lack of confidence or knowledge about how to take the next step. Usually, this hesitation leads to loss of momentum and results in plateaued church growth. Pastoral and staff leadership, knowledge, growth experience and people skills are vital to continued growth if cities are to be reached in this generation. Growth-minded churches and church leaders often look beyond their own congregation for solutions and continued fulfillment of the Great Commission mandate found in Matthew 28:19–20. Since most churches do not have a defined growth strategy based on scriptural principles, the most common result is an unplanned church split.

Growth-oriented church leaders saturate themselves with information about methods adopted by other churches that have surpassed them in growth. Perhaps the most valid reason for examining the growth of other churches is to observe how they have learned to cooperate with God in their process of growth. This examination benefits others only as it aids in the avoidance of mistakes, detours, and traps that hinder God-directed growth.

"Megachurch," as a general term used for the largest of churches in the decade of the 1980s, is examined below, as well as other new expressions being used for large churches. The definition of *mega* as being *"large"* and *"huge"* began to undergo redefinition in recent years with news of churches larger than those in the United States.

The decade of the 1960s was the time when churches began to experience explosive growth outside the United States. For churches in the United States, megachurch growth began to increase after 1970.

As mentioned earlier, the Jotabeche Methodist Pentecostal Church of Santiago, Chile, has the distinction of having been the world's largest church in the 1960s, with 40,000 members by 1965. Earlier in the decade the church broke the 10,000-worship attendance barrier and initiated a new era of church growth in the twentieth century.

The Yoido Full Gospel Church of Seoul, Korea, grew from 5 people in 1958 to 8,252 members in 1970, to 22,992 in 1975, to 133,000 members in 1980, and then to 230,000 by 1982 (a gain of almost 100,000 new members in only two years).[1] In the book *The World's 20 Largest Churches* this dramatic growth is described:

Imagine growing at a rate of more than 8,000 new members during a one-month period. By 1984 the rate of growth increased to 10,000 new members monthly.

Church reports from January, 1984, revealed a total membership of 350,000 with 316 pastoral staff members; 20,805 deacons and deaconesses; 19,839 cell groups, with attendance at the cell groups averaging 297,585; and a weekly all-night prayer service attendance of more than 12,000. Also, the total number of baptisms reported in 1980 was 12,000.[2]

By the period 1981–82, for the first time in the second millennium of the Christian church's history, at least ten churches had broken the 10,000-average weekly attendance barrier. The largest church in the United States ranked fourth among the world's largest churches. The United States church had not grown smaller, the other churches merely grew larger . . . and larger. The five churches reported as having the largest worship attendance in 1981–82 are listed below.

Table 8 Worship Attendance of the World's Largest Churches, 1981–82	
Church	*Worship Attendance*
1. Yoido Full Gospel Church Seoul, Korea	105,000
2. Jotabeche Methodist Pentecostal Church Santiago, Chile	60,000
3. Young Nak Presbyterian Church Seoul, Korea	20,000
4. First Baptist Church Hammond, Indiana	18,500
5. Calvary Chapel of Costa Mesa Santa Ana, California	12,500

Source: John N. Vaughan, *The World's 20 Largest Churches*, (Grand Rapids: Baker, 1984), 287.

Just as the Jotabeche Methodist Pentecostal Church broke the 10,000-attendance barrier in about 1960, the 20,000-attendance barrier was broken in 1975 by the Yoido Full Gospel Church. The Yoido church continued to penetrate new attendance frontiers.

Table 9 New Attendance Barriers Broken by the Yoido Full Gospel Church

Attendance	Year
20,000	1975
30,000	1976
40,000	1977
50,000	1978
60,000	1978
70,000	1979
80,000	1979
100,000	1980
200,000	1982
300,000	1984

K-Church: The Church of a Thousand

"K-Church": 1,000–1,999 average worship attendance (includes all children) or 1,000 resident (reachable) members. This author estimates the number of United States churches in this category to be about 25,000 congregations (or 5 percent of the national estimate of at least 500,000 congregations of all sizes and types).

The term "K-Church" was first used around 1987–88 by Dr. Bill Sullivan, who serves as church-growth director for the international headquarters of the Church of the Nazarene in Kansas City, Missouri. He used the term to designate Nazarene churches in the attendance and/or membership category mentioned above.

M-Church: The Church of Thousands

"Megachurch": Any church with an average weekly attendance (worship or other) of at least 2,000 people. The category includes churches of 20,000 and even 200,000 worship attendance or larger. A church may have 15,000 "members," but it must have an average attendance (worship or other) of at least 2,000 people to be classified as a megachurch.

For example, a church with 2,000 members but an average attendance of 1,500 people, is a K-Church rather than an M-Church. Likewise, as in the case of many Independent churches that have larger attendance than membership, a church with a membership of 1,500 people but an average weekly attendance of 2,000 people is an M-Church. This size congregation has been at various times included in the assigned label "superchurch"[3] and "mini-denomination."[4]

The category includes declining, plateaued, and growing churches and the dynamics contributing to their present condition. Some of these dynamics are healthy and others are infectious and pathological in character.

M^2 Church: The Church of Tens of Thousands

"Megachurch^2": A megachurch of any average weekly attendance (worship or other) of 10,000 or more people. This category also includes declining, plateaued, and growing churches along with the dynamics involved in their present condition. The dynamics leading to the present condition of a church, any size church, will be either healthy or pathological in character and may not represent an application of metachurch principles.

In 1988 C. Peter Wagner referred to Carl George's use of the term "metachurch" to describe a certain size congregation—a church with 10,000 members or larger. He described the term as the "dynamics of the transition from the megachurch (several thousands of members) to the metachurch (several tens of thousands of members).[5]

Two ingredients or definitions are being mingled in Wagner's use of the definition. First, "dynamics of . . . transition" describes a *process*. Second, "tens of thousands" describes a *product* of the process. This is much like using a term to define itself, and in the world of language invites possible confusion. The following paragraphs offer some clarification of the subject.

The term "metachurch" originally suggested by Paul Heibert, a faculty member at Trinity Evangelical Divinity School, Deerfield, Illinois, has gone through a series of changes in definition, as communicated in various forums these past five years.

Today, the term has metamorphosed beyond that simpler definition understood by most of us in its earlier days. First, it was a label for any church with more than 10,000 members. The earliest reference was merely to megachurch[2] and was a reference to church size. While some of the largest churches had been mentioned by C. Peter Wagner in his books, the first expanded list of these and other churches appeared in the "Fuller Factor" chapter of *The Complete Book of Church Growth*[6] in 1981. An updated listing of more than twenty of the world's largest churches (all with a membership of more than 12,000 people) appeared in the 1984 edition of *The World's 20 Largest Churches*. Their infrastructure ratios were included in the book.

Contrary to a claim otherwise,[7] the book also included for the first time in print a listing of thirteen of the world's largest Assemblies of God megachurches. Some national Assemblies of God leaders questioned whether they should even have been included since their structure was radically different from churches in America, Korea, and other countries.

Many people, for example, are unaware that it is common for Brazilian megachurches to have satellite mission
churches with several thousand attendance each—even located in other cities and other states. For this reason, it
seemed best to list these churches in a chapter identified
separately as "Brazil's Super Churches: Three Models." The
chapter concluded by listing the ten Assemblies reported
by Bernhard Johnson as having from 18,460 to 110,000
members.

To summarize the relationship between *megachurch* and
metachurch, the term metachurch as it relates to congregational size is the same as megachurch^2, a church with 10,000
or more in attendance. When the term refers to organizational structure, it means growing larger by structuring
small. While the term metachurch is new, the idea is not
new. The Southern Baptist Convention, for example, has
built the greatest number of large churches in North America through this concept for decades.

As early as 1949 Louis Entzminger, pastor of First Baptist Church of New Orleans before joining J. Frank Norris
at First Baptist Church of Fort Worth, wrote in his book
How to Organize and Administer a Great Sunday School about
the multiplication of groups:

> When a class of a certain age gets as many members as it
> should have—seven or eight—a new teacher should be se-
> cured. This teacher should be present whether a single new
> pupil is ready for the new class or not. . . . If the Sunday
> School is to grow, the growth of the organization will pre-
> cede the growth of the school. A growing school will be con-
> stantly adding new teachers and building up new classes.[8]

Earlier in the same text, Entzminger lists the twenty-three
churches in North America reporting the largest Sunday
schools during the decade of the 1940s. Most of these

churches were Southern Baptist congregations. He comments about the growth of these churches:

> I do not claim credit for building these twenty-three largest Sunday schools; but I claim that my work, plans and methods doubled and, in some instances, immediately tripled the attendance of these Sunday Schools.[9]

J. N. Barnette, reportedly named by Billy Graham as the most influential evangelist in the twentieth century because of his multiplication of new Sunday school classes among Southern Baptists, wrote in his 1956 book, *The Pull of the People:*

> New units grow faster, win more people to Christ and provide more workers.
> Fruit comes from new growth. Roses bloom on new growth. Without new growth there would be little fruit for food and few flowers for beauty and perfume. This law is as applicable to a Sunday school as to a fruit tree.[10]

To this day, these principles have led the Southern Baptist Convention to become the only non-Catholic denomination able to claim the largest number of megachurches and fast-growth churches in North America. The very fact that churches with more than 10,000 worship attendance are also experiencing both plateau and decline in the United States, Korea, and some third-world countries seems to establish "metachurch" as more of a small-group growth dynamic than an actual size of congregation.

When is a metachurch (i.e., size) not a metachurch (i.e., dynamics)? When a church of 10,000 or more people, or any size, is both structured for multiplication and is, in fact, multiplying, it may be considered a metachurch. However, any church, even the 10,000-plus-attendance church, fails to qualify as a true metachurch if it is either plateaued or declining. The nongrowing church may have cells or classes that are multiplying, but the church itself may not be experiencing growth by addition much less multiplication.

Perhaps, Carl George will some day recognize that metachurch is merely the dynamic of growing larger through small groups—Sunday school and/or home cell groups. George's color-coded "metaglobe" is a tool for classifying the organizations of a church but is only an extension of the more basic metachurch concept. These should not be confused as being one and the same concept. The metaglobe's "zones" are merely arenas in which growth principles are to be applied. These zones are the traditional arenas most competent church-growth consultants already consider. Fuller Institute has simply added the novelty of color to these traditional zones.

The largest home cell group churches in the world also report some of the largest Sunday schools of the world. The major difference is that space restrictions due to the extremely high cost of land (up to $9 million per acre) has led them to use on-campus classroom space for children, youth, and university students. Some churches, like the Yoido Full Gospel Church of Seoul, provide both Sunday school and home groups for children and youth.

Sunday school churches are the churches that have applied metachurch principles for decades in the emerging megachurches within the Assemblies of God and the Southern Baptist Convention. These two groups lead all others in the number of emerging megachurches and existing megachurches. The term "megachurch" is used in this text to designate a church with an average attendance of 2,000 or more individuals. This definition includes all children attending with their parents.

The metachurch concept seems new to many denominational and Independent churches because they have never understood its principles, have forgotten them, have modified them to the point of ineffectiveness, have become preoccupied with other priorities, or have, through stubbornness, refused to apply them because most growing churches are already using them.

Some critics think that the day of the Sunday school is past. This belief is based on the fact that worship attendance tends to be greater than Sunday school in multitudes of churches. Among fast-growing churches, this trend is no surprise. These churches, especially among Southern Baptist Convention and Assemblies of God churches, also have rapid-growing Sunday schools. Worship attendance now exceeds Sunday school primarily because multiple worship services require less energy in initiating new growth than Sunday school.

The Sunday school and/or home cell groups, however, are essential if new worshipers are to be assimilated for and equipped with skills and attitudes for effective discipleship and ministry.

The wise pastor of a rapid-growth church follows the instituting of additional worship services with an expanded small-group ministry. Churches that generate their worship attendance growth through the continued creation of new multiple worship services, without also creating additional small groups (i.e., Sunday school classes and/or home cell groups), are in danger of building the empty cathedrals of the next generation.

The major issue in continued growth is not merely one of small churches versus large churches. The issue is the ability of a congregation, any size congregation, to be able to reproduce itself through new groups, additional worship services, and new mission churches. The issue also leads church leaders beyond merely having small groups to developing small groups designed for, and capable of, multiplication.

Once a church's groups grow beyond sixteen people, the potential for plateau and numerical decline increases. Groups with dynamic leaders, either ordained staff or laypeople, can slow this process temporarily. However, once a group reaches sixteen to twenty people in attendance, it tends to lose both its ability and desire to reproduce.

The chemistry of the group changes, and the group becomes leader focused, curriculum-content bound, and a passive consumer of information. At this point evangelism among group members may become a topic of discussion more than a matter of lifestyle among group members. Preoccupation with nurture of internal growth replaces expansion growth, as the congregation begins to plateau and even decline numerically.

4

America's Changing Cities

The growth, plateauing, and decline of cities impacts all congregations significantly—urban, suburban, and even rural. The megachurches and their impact on family life in cities are increasingly having to come to grips with this reality. Past generations of churches, because of larger family size, were more easily able to influence the assimilation of migrant family units into city life and to influence cities through them than is possible today. Today's families are much more mobile and much smaller than in past decades. More effort, energy, and finances are required to reach the new multitude of smaller families.

Paul C. Glick, formerly with the Bureau of the Census, wrote in his article, "Family Trends in the United States, 1890 to 1940":

The first census of the United States showed that in 1790 there were more families consisting of five persons than any other number. One hundred years later, in 1890, four-person families were most numerous. By 1900, there were more three-person families and by 1930 more two-person families than any other size. In brief, the modal or typical family size, changed from five persons to two persons in the course of 140 years.[1]

Commenting on the growth of cities by population size, those under 100,000 population and those over 100,000, Glick noted, five decades ago in 1942:

> For 50 years there has been roughly the same number of families in cities under 100,000 population as over 100,000, with the smaller cities growing more slowly than the larger cities. Since 1930, however, the smaller have continued to gain faster than the country as a whole, while the larger cities have not quite held their own. Recent population growth has centered largely in the satellite cities within metropolitan districts, or in other words, in urban areas near but outside the metropolitan central cities.[2]

R. J. Johnson, in *The American Urban System*, observes that prior to World War II the development of urban systems tended to be concentrated within the higher population density of center-city cores. In the immediate post-World War II decades a reversal in the earlier pattern occurred, with migration of both households and industry into newly developing suburbs. This trend became known among sociologists and urban planners as "sprawl."[3]

According to David A. Heenan, chief executive officer of one of Hawaii's original "Big Five" companies and former faculty member at both The Wharton School and Columbia Graduate School of Business, in his book, *The New Corporate Frontier: The Big Move to Small Town, U.S.A.*, describes this exurbia trend as a "Ring of 'urban suburbs,'" that, "grew in concentric circles, forming a kind of Republican donut around the traditionally strong Democratic center city."[4] He traces this redesigning of America's large cities during the mid-1960s:

> Twenty-five years ago, New York City's commuter fringe cut across points of Long Island, Connecticut, and New Jersey at a radius of about 30 miles from the Big Apple. Later, the perimeter of the circle stretched to about 60 miles from Manhattan. Today, another ring—including Pennsylvania's northeastern border—about 80 miles from Times Square is on the fringe of New York's expanding metropolis region. Lured by lower housing prices. . . . These hearty souls brave 2-hour trips into Manhattan each day.[5]

This new manifestation of the commuter's city in urban America is reinforced by a network of more than thirty-two thousand shopping centers and malls. The commuter can exit the interstate at almost any point to buy what he needs during the two-hour trip mentioned above.

In *Megatrends 2000,* John Naisbitt and Patricia Aburdene quote Jack Lessinger, professor emeritus at the University of Washington, in his views on "penturbia" or the population centers developing beyond the traditional urban suburbs. He describes this zone of migration as "the fifth big historical U.S. migration." David A. Heenan notes, "Penturbia, the experts agree, embraces metropolitan, non-metropolitan, rural, and semirural communities."[6]

More specifically, he contends, "Typically, these cities are outlying townships of 200,000 or fewer people that are located at least 50 miles from a major city."[7] Naisbitt and Aburdene, referring to Lessinger, comment:

> It is one of the great untold stories of the 1980's and 1990's. Between one-third and one-half of the American and Canadian middle-class will live outside metropolitan and suburban areas by 2010. . . .

"The first migration," says Professor Lessinger, "was north to south from the first colonies, between 1735 and 1846; the second was west to the Mississippi-Ohio River towns, between 1789 and 1900; the third was from country to the cities, between 1846 and 1958; the fourth, beginning around 1900, was from the cities to the post-World War II suburbs, overlapping somewhat with the third."[8]

According to Heenan, this major shift has already begun to be felt by large numbers of United States companies, including Fortune 500 corporations. He noted that cities like New York City, Chicago, Pittsburgh, Detroit, and Philadelphia have already lost as many as half of their major hometown companies.

> . . . 27 percent of the Fortune 500 industrial concerns called the Big Apple home in 1960, 23 percent in 1970, 16 percent in 1980, and just 9 percent in 1990. . . .
> Almost half of greater Chicago's Fortune 500 companies are based in its suburban corridor.[9]

These more than 200 new cities beyond the larger cities, even beyond many of yesterday's suburbs, have been called "edge cities" by Joel Garreau in his book *Edge City: Life on the New Frontier*.[10]

A cover-story review of the book in *American Demographics* states, "Every single American city that is growing, is growing in the fashion of Los Angeles. It is sprouting multiple urban cores."[11] Characteristics of these more than 200 cities include: (1) each "has 5 million square feet or more of leasable office space, (2) has 600,000 square feet or more of leasable retail space, (3) more jobs than bedrooms, (4) is perceived by the population as one place, and (5) was nothing like a 'city' as recently as 30 years ago."[12] Thirteen mid-sized metropolitan areas given as examples of the "edge city" trend, where office space outside the central city exceeds that inside, include: Houston,

Boston, Dallas, Philadelphia, Denver, San Diego, Pittsburgh, St. Louis, Baltimore, Kansas City, Miami, Tampa, and New Orleans.[13] Garreau writes, "The battles we fight today over urban development have echoes back to 1956, when Dwight D. Eisenhower changed America forever with the creation of the interstate highway program."[14]

Examples of this type of city, given in the article, include the Galleria area west of downtown Houston, which is larger than downtown Minneapolis and King of Prussia, Pennsylvania, and where the exit sign on Route 202 reads, "MALL NEXT FOUR LEFTS." These high-tech, lower-density valleys and wooded areas in their first-generation form can be located ten miles from a downtown area, whereas, a second-generation variety may be located another twenty miles beyond the first.[15]

These demographic shifts, however, are part of much larger historic patterns. Church life and church attendance patterns are influenced significantly by these trends. Rural churches are left bleeding from the hemorrhage of membership losses, traditional suburbs are constantly undergoing transition, and denominations are constantly reminded of the ever-changing needs of the center cities of urban America. Few congregations are left untouched. The population and social dynamics of the nation's metropolitan centers pose no small challenge to both congregations and denominations.

Jerome P. Cavanaugh, former mayor of Detroit, gives a graphic overview of the rapid rate of change in American life since the beginning of the twentieth century:

> In 1900, there were 36 million people living in cities and towns of 2,500 population or over, and in 1967 that number was 175 million. This is an increase from 47 percent to 87 percent of the total population. . . .The suburban population doubled from 1940 to 1960, an increase from 27 to

55 million persons, while the central cities increased only from 46 to 58 million, or 27 percent.[16]

. . . Agricultural improvements . . . from 1931 to 1965 doubled the yield of wheat per acre from 13 to 27 bushels and tripled corn production from 23 to 73 bushels per acre, [making] it possible for 4.86 percent of our workers to feed . . . our 200 million population. . . .[17] From a nation of dirt roads and coal stoves in 1900, we have evolved into a nation with indoor plumbing, refrigerators, electric household appliances, running water, air conditioning and central heat.[18]

In 1900, only 280,000 of our young people were enrolled in universities, while in 1967 there were over seven million. . . . The number of college students in the United States is more than double the 2,500,000 in all of Western Europe.[19]

Measured by today's United States government guidelines, an "urban area" should have a population of at least one thousand people per square mile and a total population of at least fifty thousand people.[20] Metropolitan areas must have at least fifty thousand population up to and including special designations of a million or more people.[21] According to *American Demographics,* "The 1990 census added 33 new urbanized areas. . . . The 396 urbanized areas in the U.S. include all 284 officially designated metropolitan areas, but none of the 33 newly designated areas is a metropolitan area."[22] "The U.S. population grew by less than 1 percent annually between 1980 and 1990, while the average metro grew by 1.1 percent. Metropolitan areas were home to 77 percent of Americans on Census Day last year, up from 76 percent in 1980."[23]

Twenty percent of United States cities declined in population during the decade of the 1980s. Another 65 percent grew slowly, while almost 23 percent experienced rapid growth.

Of the 320 officially designated metropolitan areas, [note: excludes the new areas mentioned above] 65 actually lost population between 1980 and 1990. Another 116 metros grew more slowly than the 10 percent rate for the national population. Only 73 metros increased by 20 percent or more in ten years. The 1990's promise even slower growth. The U.S. population should grow only 7 percent in the next decade, says the Census Bureau.[24]

According to noted urban planners, today's metropolitan cities have evolved into urban empires with marked differences from other traditional cities. Hans Blumenfeld, in *The Modern Metropolis: Its Origins, Growth, Characteristics, and Planning,* identifies six distinctive traits. He summarizes these as (1) central leadership, (2) population up to ten times that of the largest preindustrial city, (3) modern transportation, which increases its commuting radius about tenfold, or up to 100 times larger than the largest cities of former times, (4) its blend of both rural and urban districts rather than simple being one or the other, (5) its segregation of work place from residence, and (6) high worker mobility and choices in job selection.[25]

Cities and the Churches

America's cities are each unique in their mix of churches. This mix of churches is identifiable to observers in at least six ways. Major sources for church information in each metropolitan area include: (1) the area telephone book, (2) occasional directories published by local council of churches, (3) national yearbooks published by each major and many smaller denominations, (4) direct-mailing list companies, (5) a publication produced each decade, *Churches and Church Membership in the U.S.,* as denominational statisticians share information, and (6) special research projects such as "The National Survey of Religious Identification 1989–90" by the Graduate School and University Center of the City University of New York. Each source of infor-

mation, as listed, is progressively more complex and re-
moved from the common citizen.

Cities vary in the total number of churches, the variety
of denominational groups, and the number, type, size, and
growth rate of megachurches. All of the descriptions of the
city given above are for the purpose of intensifying our
awareness of the gigantic task facing today's churches.

Shown in Table 10 are the 50 largest cities in the United
States and the number of churches reported by city officials for the *Information Please Almanac, Atlas & Yearbook*.[26]
Population is based on 1990 United States government
census data for population inside the primary central city,
as listed in the fourth edition of the *State Metropolitan Area
Data Book 1991*.[27] The church-to-population ratio and
churches per square mile are calculated by the author based
on the above two sources.

Information on the fifty largest cities in the United States
and their church-to-church population and church-per-
square mile ratios is given in the following tables.

Table 10 Total Number of Churches
in the 50 Largest U.S. Cities, 1990

No. of Churches	City	No. of Churches	City
3525	New York, N.Y.	1018	Philadelphia, Pa.
2000	Los Angeles, Calif.	941	Fort Worth, Tex.
1974	Dallas, Tex.	932	Denver, Colo.
1750	Houston, Tex.	900	St. Louis, Mo.
1500	Atlanta, Ga.	850	Cincinnati, Ohio
1256	Detroit, Mich.	824	Jacksonville, Fla.
1220	Cleveland, Ohio	802	Nashville, Tenn.
1200	Indianapolis, Ind.	800	Memphis, Tenn.
1153	Chicago, Ill.	768	Oklahoma City, Okla.
1100	Kansas City, Mo.	751	Washington, D.C.
1100	Buffalo, N.Y.	703	Portland, Ore.

699*	San Antonio, Tex.	412	Charlotte, N.C.
644	New Orleans, La.	411	Milwaukee, Wis.
631	Tulsa, Okla.	408	San Diego, Calif.
584	Seattle, Wash.	403	San Jose, Calif.
579	Sacramento, Calif.	400	Honolulu, Hawaii
567†	Phoenix, Ariz.	387	Boston, Mass.
540	San Francisco, Calif.	382	El Paso, Tex.
531	Columbus, Ohio	374	Oakland, Calif.
488	Pittsburgh, Pa.	353	Austin, Tex.
466	Baltimore, Md.	294	Omaha, Nebr.
458	Toledo, Ohio	274	Miami, Fla.
450	Fresno, Calif.	236	Long Beach, Calif.
439	Tucson, Ariz.	211	Albuquerque, N.M.
419	Minneapolis, Minn.	171	Virginia Beach , Va.

Sources: With the exceptions noted, information on the number of churches was provided by each of the cities for the *Information Please Almanac Atlas and Yearbook,* 45th ed. (Boston: Houghton Mifflin, 1992), 773–83. Used by permission.

* *San Antonio Yellow Pages,* Southwestern Bell Media, Spring 1989–1990, 289–98.

† *Phoenix Yellow Pages, U.S. West Direct,* March 1991–1992, 571–87.

Table 11 Churches Per Square Mile in the 50 Largest U.S. Cities, 1990

Churches per square mile	City	Churches per square mile	City
26	Buffalo, N.Y.	8	Philadelphia, Pa.
15	St. Louis, Mo.	7	Oakland, Calif.
15	Cleveland, Ohio	6	Toledo, Ohio
12	San Francisco, Calif.	6	Sacramento, Calif.
11	Washington, D.C.	6	Denver, Colo.
11	Cincinnati, Ohio	6	Baltimore, Md.
11	Atlanta, Ga.	5	Fresno, Calif.
11	New York, N.Y.	5	Portland, Ore.
9	Detroit, Mich.	5	Dallas, Tex.
9	Pittsburgh, Pa.	5	Chicago, Ill.
8	Minneapolis, Minn.	5	Long Beach, Calif.
8	Boston, Mass.	4	Seattle, Wash.
8	Miami, Fla.	4	Kansas City, Mo.

4	Los Angeles, Calif.	2	Charlotte, N.C.
4	Milwaukee, Wis.	2	Nashville, Tenn.
3	Austin, Tex.	2	San Jose, Calif.
3	Houston, Tex.	2	Albuquerque, N.M.
3	Tucson, Ariz.	2	El Paso, Tex.
3	New Orleans, La.	2	San Antonio, Tex.
3	Memphis, Tenn.	1	Honolulu, Hawaii
3	Indianapolis, Ind.	1	Jacksonville, Fla.
3	Tulsa, Okla.	1	Oklahoma City, Okla.
3	Fort Worth, Tex.	1	Virginia Beach, Va.
3	Columbus, Ohio	1	Phoenix, Ariz.
3	Omaha, Nebr.	1	San Diego, Calif.

Sources: Calculations by John N. Vaughan based on the 1990 U.S. Government Census population data for the primary central city as listed in the *State and Metropolitan Area Data Book 1991,* 4th ed. (Washington, D.C.: U.S. Government Printing Office, 1991).

Table 12 Churches per Population of the 50 Largest U.S. Cities, 1990

Church to Population Ratio	City	Church to Population Ratio	City
1:2414	Chicago, Ill.	1:1308	Miami, Fla.
1:2299	Virginia Beach, Va.	1:1239	Columbus, Ohio
1:2077	New York, N.Y.	1:1158	Philadelphia, Pa.
1:1941	San Jose, Calif.	1:1142	Omaha, Nebr.
1:1823	Albuquerque, N.M.	1:995	Oakland, Calif.
1:1820	Long Beach, Calif.	1:980	Austin, Tex.
1:1743	Los Angeles, Calif.	1:940	Charlotte, N.C.
1:1734	Phoenix, Ariz.	1:932	Houston, Tex.
1:1589	San Diego, Calif.	1:923	Tucson, Ariz.
1:1579	Baltimore, Md.	1:913	Honolulu, Hawaii
1:1528	Milwaukee, Wis.	1:884	Seattle, Wash.
1:1484	Boston, Mass.	1:879	Minneapolis, Minn.
1:1349	El Paso, Tex.	1:818	Detroit, Mich.
1:1341	San Francisco, Calif.	1:816	Jacksonville, Fla.
1:1308	San Antonio, Tex.	1:808	Washington, D.C.

1:787	Fresno, Calif.	1:579	Oklahoma City, Okla.
1:772	New Orleans, La.	1:510	Dallas, Tex.
1:763	Memphis, Tenn.	1:502	Denver, Colo.
1:758	Pittsburgh, Pa.	1:476	Fort Worth, Tex.
1:727	Toledo, Ohio	1:441	St. Louis, Mo.
1:637	Nashville, Tenn.	1:428	Cincinnati, Ohio
1:622	Sacramento, Calif.	1:414	Cleveland, Ohio
1:622	Portland, Ore.	1:396	Kansas City, Mo.
1:620	Indianapolis, Ind.	1:298	Buffalo, N.Y.
1:582	Tulsa, Okla.	1:263	Atlanta, Ga.

Sources: Calculations by John N. Vaughan based on the 1990 U.S. Government Census population data for the primary central city as listed in the *State and Metropolitan Area Data Book 1991,* 4th ed. (Washington, D.C.: U.S. Government Printing Office, 1991).

Table 13 50 Largest Cities in the U.S., Their Population and Churches, 1990

City	Number of Churches	Pop. per Sq. Mile	No. of Churches per Sq. Mile	Church to Pop. Ratio in City
Albuquerque, N.M.	211	2,849	2	1:1823
Atlanta, Ga.	1,500	2,897	11	1:263
Austin, Tex.	353	4,013	3	1:980
Baltimore, Md.	466	9,200	6	1:1579
Boston, Mass.	387	12,218	8	1:1484
Buffalo, N.Y.	1,100	7,812	26	1:298
Charlotte, N.C.	421	2,262	2	1:940
Chicago, Ill.	1,153	12,209	5	1:2414
Cincinnati, Ohio	850	4,667	11	1:428
Cleveland, Ohio	1,220	6,400	15	1:414
Columbus, Ohio	511	3,229	3	1:1239
Dallas, Tex.	1,974	2,663	5	1:510
Denver, Colo.	932	3,035	6	1:502
Detroit, Mich.	1,256	7,188	9	1:818
El Paso, Tex.	382	2,086	2	1:1349
Fort Worth, Tex.	941	1,517	3	1:476
Fresno, Calif.	450	3,577	5	1:787

Honolulu, Hawaii	400	608	1	1:913
Houston, Tex.	1,750	2,806	3	1:932
Indianapolis, Ind.	1,200	2,116	3	1:620
Jacksonville, Fla.	824	886	1	1:816
Kansas City, Mo.	1,100	1,372	4	1:396
Long Beach, Calif.	236	8,783	5	1:1820
Los Angeles, Calif.	2,000	7,463	4	1:1743
Memphis, Tenn.	800	2,172	3	1:763
Miami, Fla.	274	10,545	8	1:1308
Milwaukee, Wis.	411	6,611	4	1:1528
Minneapolis, Minn.	419	6,697	8	1:879
Nashville/Davidson, Tenn.	802	958	2	1:637
New Orleans, La.	644	2,497	3	1:772
New York, N.Y.	3,525	23,320	11	1:2077
Oakland, Calif.	374	6,893	7	1:995
Oklahoma City, Okla.	768	713	1	1:579
Omaha, Nebr.	294	3,293	3	1:1142
Philadelphia, Pa.	1,018	11,658	8	1:1158
Phoenix, Ariz.	567*	2,308	1	1:1734
Pittsburgh, Pa.	488	6,725	9	1:758
Portland, Ore.	703	3,192	5	1:622
Sacramento, Calif.	579	3,192	6	1:622
St. Louis, Mo.	900	6,503	15	1:441
San Antonio, Tex.	699†	2,744	2	1:1339
San Diego, Calif.	408	3,365	1	1:1589
San Francisco, Calif.	540	15,738	12	1:1341
San Jose, Calif.	403	4,521	2	1:1941
Seattle, Wash.	584	3,585	4	1:884
Toledo, Ohio	458	3,963	6	1:727
Tucson, Ariz.	439	2,598	3	1:923
Tulsa, Okla.	631	1,913	3	1:582
Virginia Beach, Va.	171	1,517	1	1:2299
Washington, D.C.	751	8,925	11	1:808

Phoenix Yellow Pages, U.S. West Direct, March 1991–1992, 571–87.
† *San Antonio Yellow Pages*, Southwestern Bell Media, Spring 1989–1990, 289–98.
Calculations by John N. Vaughan.

Church-planting strategist's eyes will immediately gravitate to the far-right column—the church-to-population-ratio column. For America to be evangelized, churches of all sizes must become increasingly aware of the degree to which each metropolitan area and county of the nation has or has not been evangelized. The above ratios include congregations of all types—the most fundamental and also non-Christian congregations. This immediately increases the number of people in the population still unreached by the born-again, biblical Christians per church to a level above that indicated in the ratios.

The Home Mission Board for the Southern Baptist Convention has developed an "evangelism index" and each decade applies a formula to the total number of churches in each county. The index is weighted theologically to identify the potential biblically born-again population in each county of the nation. This approach evaluates more than the churched or unchurched percentage of the general population.

While all New Testament churches must excel in their pastoral-ministry roles, the churches that will continue to thrive and capture the hearts and souls of urban America will be those with intense missionary vision and skills. Make no mistake about the magnitude of the challenge and opportunity: America's cities, and even her villages, are still missionary turf.

Churches must continue to redefine, redream, and retake the multitudes living in plateaued, declining, and ever-changing communities and cities, as well as the new cities described in this chapter. America's megachurches and emerging megachurches are uniquely equipped to meet today's challenges. They are like God's magnets among the multitudes.

5

Urban Megachurches

The names of cities associated with the growth of large churches have changed radically since the founding of America. Prior to 1900, the nation's largest churches were usually located in New York City, Brooklyn, Philadelphia, Boston, Chicago, and Detroit. In *The Large Membership Church,* Warren J. Hartman and Robert L. Wilson refer to early growth among Methodist churches:

> The very large churches had not developed by the turn of the century. A large number of Methodist congregations with between 200 and 400 members were located in the major cities. Philadelphia had no Methodist church over 776 members and only four congregations out of 92 had over 700 members. New York had only one large church. Similar patterns existed in Chicago and Detroit. In 1900 Detroit had only

two large Methodist congregations, the largest with 960 members. Detroit's growth was to come later with the development of the auto industry. Chicago had six large churches with memberships ranging from 739 to 2906.[1]

These authors note that widespread development of public transportation by 1925 led to the rise of suburban congregations. Racially changing communities during the 1950s led many inner-city white congregations to relocate to the newly developing suburban neighborhoods.

By the mid 1980's the large white congregations were in the more remote suburbs. Only two United Methodist churches in Chicago had more than 1,000 members. Only one church in Detroit, two in Philadelphia, and four in New York had over 1,000 members. Of these eight churches, six are black.[2]

Table 14 Number of Churches in 20 Largest U.S. Cities, 1990, with Comparative Figures for 1890.

	City	1890	1990	Net Gain
1.	New York, N.Y.	644	3525	2881
2.	Los Angeles, Calif.	62	2000	1938
3.	Dallas, Tex.	55	1974	1919
4.	Houston, Tex.	52	1750	1698
5.	Atlanta, Ga.	92	1500	1408
6.	Detroit, Mich.	152	1256	1104
7.	Cleveland, Ohio	190	1220	1030
8.	Indianapolis, Ind.	105	1200	1095
9.	Chicago, Ill.	573	1153	580
10.	Kansas City, Mo./Kans.	165	1100	935
11.	Buffalo, N.Y.	156	1100	944
12.	Philadelphia, Pa.	610	1018	408
13.	Fort Worth, Tex.	—	—	—
14.	Denver, Colo.	98	932	834
15.	St. Louis, Mo.	289	900	611

16.	Cincinnati, Ohio	179	850	671
17.	Jacksonville, Fla.	—	824	—
18.	Nashville, Tenn.	101	802	701
19.	Memphis, Tenn.	51	800	749
20.	Oklahoma City, Okla.	—	768	—

Sources: Population of the United States, 11th Census: 1890. Part 1. (Government Printing Office, 1895), 91. The 1990 information was provided by each city for *Information Please Almanac Atlas and Yearbook*, 45th ed. (Boston: Houghton Mifflin, 1992), 773–83. Used by permission.

Net gain calculations by John N. Vaughan.

Elmer L. Towns's book *The Ten Largest Sunday Schools,* in 1969, indicated that the large non-Catholic congregations were still concentrated basically in the eastern half of the nation. Large churches, he reported, were located in the five eastern states of Michigan (Detroit), Indiana (Hammond), Ohio (Akron, Canton, and Cincinnati), Virginia (Lynchburg), and Tennessee (Chattanooga). The other three churches were located in Texas (Dallas), Colorado (Denver), and California (Van Nuys).

Except for the three Independent Baptist congregations in Ohio, all of the other churches were scattered and isolated from other large congregations. These ten churches ranged in Sunday school attendance from 2,453 at Calvary Temple in Denver to 5,762 at Akron Baptist Temple in Akron, Ohio.

In 1986, *Church Growth Today* newsletter reported that newly emerging megachurches with an average annual worship attendance net gain of 500 or more people during 1985–1986 were to be found in Denver (5), Dallas (4), Atlanta (4), Los Angeles (5), Phoenix (2), Oklahoma City (2), and Chicago (2). The publication noted:

> Forty-two of the fast growth churches (76 percent of the 57 churches) are located in 19 metropolitan areas identified by *INC.* Magazine (April, 1987) as the nation's 50 fastest growing cities . . . . None of the 57 congregations were located in cities identified by *INC.* as the slowest growing metro areas.[3]

Critics of large churches need to be aware that the rise and decline of these churches during this century has been accompanied by a parallel movement of church planting. A comparison, shown in table 14, of the twenty United States cities with the largest number of congregations in 1990 with the number of congregations reported in the same cities by the 1890 United States Census illustrates the degree of the increase. Information is omitted for Fort Worth, Jacksonville, and Oklahoma City because of lack of information in the census. Some denominational groups were more aggressive in the planting of new churches than others.

During the year 1991 nearly twice as many churches may have been planted, either intentionally or as church splits, than were disbanded. American Business Directories of Omaha, Nebraska, reported in a letter to customers that 15,142 new church names were added to their records while 7,149 went "out of business" during that year.

Urban Clusters

The clustering of megachurches in urban centers has been a trend since about 1970. Factors contributing to this development since 1970 are discussed in other chapters of this book.

A brief summary of specific cities and their surrounding area that currently have clusters of megachurches might be helpful (see table 15). A megachurch, again, is any church with an average weekly worship or Sunday school attendance of at least 2,000 people. Megachurch attendance includes all children brought by their attending families. The following examples provide only a partial listing of megachurches in the model cities. Attendance information is for 1990. "Affiliation" in some instances indicates a loose fellowship of autonomous churches rather than a denomination. An example of this is the Calvary Chapel fellowship of congregations related to Calvary Chapel of Costa Mesa, California.

Table 15 Some Urban Clusters of Megachurches

Congregation	Attendance	Affiliation
Albuquerque, New Mexico		
Calvary Chapel	5,700	Calvary Chapels
Victory Love Fellowship	2,600	Independent Charismatic
Hoffmantown Baptist Church	2,354	Southern Baptist Convention
Atlanta, Georgia		
Mount Paran Church of God	9,175	Church of God— Cleveland
Chapel Hill Harvester	7,400	Independent Charismatic
Peachtree Presbyterian Church	5,800	Presbyterian Church, U.S.A.
World Changers	4,800	Independent Charismatic
Mount Ephraim Baptist Church	4,800	National Baptist Convention
First Baptist Church	4,680	Southern Baptist Convention
Roswell Street Baptist Church	4,500	Southern Baptist Convention
Dallas, Texas		
First Baptist Church	7,625*	Southern Baptist Convention
Prestonwood Baptist Church	4,120	Southern Baptist Convention
Concord Baptist Church	3,500	National Baptist (NBCA)
Fellowship Bible Church	2,240	Bible—Independent
Oak Cliff Bible Church	2,200	Bible—Independent
Chicago, Illinois		
Willow Creek Community Church	13,040	Independent
Christ Church/Oak Brook	3,300	Independent
Faith Tabernacle Church	3,200	Independent Charismatic
Homewood Full Gospel Church	2,500	Independent Charismatic
Trinity United Church	2,400	United Church of Christ
Los Angeles, California		
Calvary Chapel, Costa Mesa	12,000	Calvary Chapels
Harvest Fellowship	8,000	Calvary Chapels
Grace Community, Sun Valley	8,000	Bible—Independent
West Angeles Church of God	7,500	Church of God in Christ
Calvary Church, Santa Ana	7,123	Independent

Crystal Cathedral	6,621	Reformed Church in America
Calvary Chapel, West Covina	6,000	Calvary Chapels
Crenshaw Christian Center	6,000	Independent-Charismatic

* Includes satellite locations
©1993 John N. Vaughan

Each metropolitan area has its own unique theological blend of churches. This mosaic distinguishes each city from all others. In each setting the degree of awareness of and/or willingness to cooperate among the churches varies. The purpose in sharing these examples is merely to demonstrate the uniqueness of each urban center and to show that each is composed of a cluster of megachurches. Whereas a single megachurch ministry might have existed during earlier decades, this is not usually the case today. The urban centers of the nation have several strong and significant megachurches that each offer unique ministries and voices to address the biblical, social, and other needs of their cities.

Their ultimate test will be at the judgment seat of Jesus Christ as he judges their faithfulness to his biblical mandate to be true and faithful witnesses of him, his death, and resurrection. There are definite differences at various points of biblical doctrine among these churches. Each, however, understands itself to maintain a high view of the Bible and its authority in matters of conversion, the churches, and Christian ministry.

6

Predictable Changes in Growing Churches

Unplanned change can be the source of trauma in the life of a church, as well as of awe and gratitude. Even when a pastor dreams about growth, he may be dramatically unprepared when his church begins to grow. Visitors and new members are often added in geometrical proportion rather than by mere addition.

Calvary Chapel of Costa Mesa, California, is one of the five largest congregations in the United States. In their book *The Reproducers,* Chuck Smith and Hugh Steven write:

> The traffic . . . came not from the three hundred people the church was designed to hold, but from the hundreds that crowded into the chapel during the following months. Chuck designed the church to hold three

81

hundred never dreaming it would ever be completely filled. He believed an average attendance of approximately two hundred seventy was an ideal congregation.[1]

Many pastors of growing churches can identify with both the wonder and discomfort that must have gone through Chuck Smith's mind and heart. Several other California churches experienced dramatic growth of the kind described above during that same era. Other details of the continued growth at Calvary Chapel are noted in the book *The World's 20 Largest Churches.*

> Within five weeks of the move into a 300-seat auditorium on the first Sunday in June, 1969, Pastor Chuck Smith decided to begin a second worship service. Capacity crowds by mid-1971 led to a third morning service.
>
> By November, 1971, the chapel bought eleven acres of land for $300,000. Immediately, a 90' x 180' tent was raised to accommodate the regular crowds of 1,400 people.
>
> Before their present 2,500-seat sanctuary could be completed, the church again had to hold a second, and third, service.[2]

In 1988, Monica Hill, the editor of *British Church Growth Bulletin,* asked me to write an article outlining the predictable changes that are necessary if a church plans to grow larger. The following nineteen indicators commonly found among growing churches are given as a partial list.

1. Scheduling and Structure

The ability of a church to grow larger is directly related to its willingness and ability to open its doors beyond the weekly worship service at least one more time on Sunday and/or at other times. This gesture to the unchurched and other outsiders serves as an open invitation to explore the power of a changed life.

Churches lacking this willingness tend to see no need to add additional worship services and lack the faith to believe that the sanctuary could possibly be filled with interested people. Church leaders who are willing, but fearful, should invite God to show them how it can be accomplished (James 1:3–8). Growing churches refuse to allow the proverbial shoe to dictate how large the foot can grow.

Recently, while dining in a local restaurant, I asked the waitress how many different groups of customers she served lunch each day. Her answer was "about five or six." People begin to come about eleven o'clock and others continue to come as late as two o'clock. The restaurant offers the same service and the same menu, without compromise, to all their customers. If lunch was served just once, at eleven o'clock or noon, the restaurant would be serving only 20 percent of its present customers. Parking would be a severe problem, seating would be inadequate, and needs would remain unmet.

Today's megachurches, and emerging megachurches, continue to grow because they are learning to utilize time and space to maximum advantage. They are making these changes while still meeting the needs of multitudes in an uncompromising manner. Critics are oftentimes uninformed of the sacrifice these churches are willing to make to reach people for the gospel.

2. Pastoral Leadership

Members of small churches and even the pastor himself often expect the pastor to be available at all times, for almost all occasions and needs, and to any member or unchurched person. This demand for constant availability of the pastor minimizes the Lord's expectations that the sheep be equipped in shepherding ministry skills.

Growing churches tend to have pastors who, as sheep themselves, are accountable to God. They must recognize their own limits in time and ministry resources (Exod. 18:13–26). Pastors of growing churches purposefully establish balance between availability and the need for competency in ministry and the pulpit. This is accomplished through time alone with God and time alone with both staff and lay shepherds, who multiply his ministry through their own.

3. Delegation

Pastors of churches that remain small tend to center most of the church's ministry, whether intentionally or unintentionally, on themselves. This practice is partially due to a perceived expectation from members and leaders of the congregation.

However, the pastor of a larger growing church increasingly releases ministry to the members. His primary role becomes one of identifying needs and enlisting ministers from within the congregation. This decision allows the church to organize its energies and influence to meet existing and potential needs (2 Tim. 2:2).

4. Decision-Making Process

Maintaining a strong claim on the right to assert member rule, even when it divides the church tends to characterize smaller congregations. As a church grows beyond being a single-cell organism and as organizational change occurs, an increasing shift in congregational polity evolves from congregational (people led), to presbyterial (deacon/staff led), to episcopal (staff/deacon led or staff led). This shift is seen in the Book of Acts and occurs in the dynamic of changing group size.

Such a shift tends to occur when a church first reaches a staff level of four or five full-time members. The prime reason for this change is the need for staff members to plan in concert and to avoid duplication in recommendations to lay committees. When staff members fail to coordinate their planning, the potential for conflict increases among themselves. Such conflict should be resolved at the staff level before it needlessly spills over into a committee of laymen.

For example, leadership enlistment is always a continuing challenge in growing churches and is compounded in plateaued churches. Staff and lay leaders can easily find that they want to enlist the same person for more than one position simultaneously. Turf conflicts and hidden-agenda problems can create stress because of what is seemingly a "too many needs" for "too few leaders" situation. While this condition cannot be totally avoided, proper staff planning becomes necessary if reckless and unnecessary conflict is to be avoided. Fruit of the Spirit and gifts of the Spirit are in delicate balance while also remaining in constructive tension.

5. Staff Enlistment

The church that remains small will have a limited number of staff members—often only the pastor. Staff members in small congregations (fewer than 200 in worship attendance) are usually like general practitioners. Churches that grow larger, however, increasingly add staff members who are specialists in a narrower area of ministry. This increase in specialization is a direct result of the increase in worship attendance.

Research for the book *The World's 20 Largest Churches* revealed that the world's largest congregations tend to add additional staff members as each increment of 150 people is added to the church. Staff disloyalty, poor staff selection, jealousy of the new staff person by the pastor, or personnel policies and practice that make staff members accountable to the committee rather than to the pastor can hinder confident and effective staff member enlistment for continued church growth.

6. Leadership Enlistment

While it may be common in churches that remain small for the pastor to enlist "opposition" leaders for fear of being accused of stacking committees with only those who agree with him, the pastor and leaders of larger growing churches tend to enlist supportive models among leaders without apology. Purposeful exclusion of lay leaders who are known for their opposition to pastor/staff leadership and congregational goals is much more common in churches that grow larger. While leaders enlisted in growing churches are not blind followers, they are usually aggressive and positive supporters.

Denominations that find this exclusion to be a problem have four basic choices: (1) discouraging churches from growing larger, (2) encouraging the larger churches to become independent congregations without affiliation to the denomination, (3) negotiating and attempting to establish a level of mutual cooperation and agreement between these churches and the denomination, or (4) ignoring the challenge and hoping that a confrontation can be avoided.

Since the population of America will only be evangelized and involved in the life of its churches by (1) existing churches growing larger, (2) the planting of tens of thousands of new congregations, or (3) a combination of these two strategies, it is unlikely that the failure to build larger churches is practical or realistic.

7. Loss of Members

Loss of members can be a serious crisis for any church. The small church, however, is especially vulnerable. Small churches, therefore, tend to avoid member loss at all costs. This often allows power groups of either families or individuals within the smaller church to influence decisions that can perpetuate nongrowth attitudes, structures, leaders, methods, and even selective membership enlistment. These forces reinforce the role of the pastor as maintainer rather than as a dynamic spiritual leader able to lead in initiating needed Bible-centered change.

The pain of change is often minimized by the smaller nongrowing congregation by managing a rapid rate of "uninvited change" at the front door. This "management" process provides a degree of predictable rate of change and loss through the back door. While the homogeneous nature of most small churches creates a climate somewhat like one big family seated to share a common family meal at a relative's home, outsiders are often viewed as "guests" who may only be passing through rather than sharing the privileges of "family" at the table.

This practice may be vividly illustrated in small churches located in stable small towns. Many of the values are simply "understood" unless you are an outsider with no appreciation for values commonly treasured in the community. "Outsider" may refer to anyone with fewer than three or four generations of relatives in the community.

These practices may hinder the growth of existing churches or the intentional planting of new churches in the small town or community in any city. It should be recognized that these "understood" values form the social bonding that allows the small church to endure over time.

The challenge, however, lies in the fact that both small and large churches are almost always located in counties where half of the population claims membership in none of the churches. Again, the focus should be placed on the major issue of a church's ability to reproduce rather than the issue of small churches versus large churches. A sick body is ineffective whether it be a small one or large one. The central issue remains the unchanging nature of the Great Commission mandate of Jesus to his churches in Matthew 28:19–20.

Pastors of churches that grow larger tend to be more willing to lose members who disagree with the procedures or philosophy of ministry of the voted will of the congregation. Some members who leave the church may feel that the equivalent of a corporate hostile takeover occurred with the coming of the new pastor.

Assuming that adequate communication took place between the new pastor and the congregation at the time of the call to serve, the new pastor usually views his leadership as compatible with the congregation's invitation to lead in positive change. Obviously, great discernment is needed by both the pastor, his staff, lay leaders, and the congregation, when such change is initiated.

When change is initiated after a period of more than three years from the date of a pastor's call to lead a church, the principles for change may be the same, but the potential for conflict may be greater. By then, congregational leadership may allow a pastor literally to risk his ministry to initiate necessary change that they are themselves unwilling to initiate. Ministry becomes a high-risk venture when this is the case and requires much prayer and sensitivity by both pastor and people. Members and friends who leave may perceive the pastor who initiated the change as a "dictator." This may or may not be a justified accusation.

Growing congregations tend to hold members more loosely and even encourage those who feel led to leave to do so with the blessing of the congregation. This is not to imply that growing churches expect less of their members. Some studies indicate that a significant dynamic of growing churches is the high expectations clearly defined for their members and potential members.

8. Evangelism Priority

Churches that remain small tend to major on winning and reaching immediate relatives, with some focus on reaching friends. More attention, though not all, is usually placed on revival evangelism than on the personal evangelism that provides the opportunity for conversion.

A 1991 study by the Home Mission Board of the Southern Baptist Convention evaluated one thousand of the denomination's forty thousand congregations. Eighty-four of the churches were identified as "high baptism churches," ninety-one others were identified as "low baptism churches, and the remaining congregations were classified as "middle baptism churches."

Churches baptizing five or more people per one hundred resident members for two consecutive years were identified as "high baptism churches" while those baptizing one or less per one hundred resident members during the same two-year period were recognized as "low baptism churches." The Baptist Press article reported:

> The research shows churches with high baptism rates have the following characteristics: a pastor who is committed to frequent personal witnessing, witness training for lay people of all ages, a variety of evangelistic methods, a vision for potential for growth and a method to identify and visit evangelistic prospects. . . .
>
> One characteristic of low baptism churches is relying on revivals for the primary evangelistic thrust. Pastors of low baptism churches tended to agree with statements such as "revivals are more important in our church than any other evangelistic effort."
>
> Pastors of high baptism churches preferred a variety of evangelistic tools.[3]

Churches that grow larger usually give priority to friendship or life-style evangelism, while not neglecting kinship evangelism. They also increasingly direct their attention and limited resources of time, finances, and people toward evangelizing specific target groups of unchurched people.

9. Tenure and Ministry Skills

Pastors of small churches tend to change congregations more frequently than those in churches that grow larger. Such mobility can reduce the ability to develop the confidence in ministry skills associated with longevity.

Pastors and staff members of churches that grow larger usually have developed ministry skills needed to cross barriers that repeatedly hinder the growth of smaller churches. While the pastors of nongrowing churches sometimes request information helpful to the growth of the church, leaders of larger growth churches usually have a corresponding willingness to share help selectively with those sincerely requesting help.

Chip Alford, in a recent issue of the Southern Baptist Convention publication *Facts & Trends,* provided the following update on pastoral tenure for his denomination:

> The latest statistics, garnered from the 1991 Uniform Church Letter, show the average pastoral tenure in the SBC is 5.5 years. A 4.3 average was reported in 1975. It rose to 4.6 years in 1980, and to 5.1 years in 1985.
>
> But since the "average" figures include extremely long tenures . . . denominational statistics specialist Jim Lowry of the Board's Corporate Planning and Research Department said a better gauge might be the "median" pastoral tenure—the middle value when half the cases are above and half are below. The number stood at 2.6 years in 1975, 2.7 years in 1980, 3.1 years in 1985 and 3.4 years in 1991. . . .
>
> The number of large churches in the SBC is increasing and pastors tend to remain longer in larger churches. Norris Smith, church staff support consultant at the Sunday School Board, said factors in longer tenure at larger churches include better salaries, increased visibility and influence in the denomination, and help from multi-member church staff.
>
> The most recent statistic on forced terminations— according to research conducted by the Sunday School

Board in 1988—showed 116 pastors being fired each month by Southern Baptist congregations. . . . "I don't see any sign of these numbers decreasing," Smith said.[4]

10. Innovation versus Imitation

Since there are many more small churches, there are also many more models of ministry available to the small churches, including both small and larger churches.

As a congregation grows larger, however, the number of effective models of ministry decrease dramatically since there are few churches with more than 500 people in worship attendance. Whereas the smaller congregation may find an abundance of creative models to imitate, it must depend more vitally upon Spirit-led innovation in ministry since the congregation is more visible to critics and media when it makes poor decisions. A smaller congregation can make a poor, even costly, decision and oftentimes few will even be aware of the mistake.

Everett M. Rogers in *Diffusion of Innovations* indicates that only 2.5 percent of any given audience are innovators. Another 13.5 percent are classified as "early adopters."[5] While the innovators are developers, this second group serves as the first-wave consumers and function as the consumer-protection reference bureau to more hesitant consumers.

This writer's opinion is that church leaders in these two categories can be found as staff members of both rapid-growing churches of all sizes and megachurches. If the pastor is not an innovator, it becomes essential to enlist staff members able to select wisely among innovations being adopted by other large churches. These staff members can often be found among the first-wave registrants for growth seminars. They are soon followed by the next 34 percent, who compose the group known as the "early majority." These leaders are cautious consumers who depend on the early adopters to screen ideas and products.

11. Planning Ahead

Focusing on the immediate tends to characterize the church that remains small. Planning is almost always short-range and a larger percentage of decisions are made informally.

However, in larger growth churches the planning process includes short-range, intermediate and long-range plans. Planning tends to be conducted in a much more formal and public manner.

12. The Learning Process

Since growth is often related to the community cultural climate as well as to pastoral leadership skills, the special knowledge of how a congregation grows can be as much caught as taught. While pastors and members of small churches tend to attend training seminars at off-site locations, pastors of larger churches tend to lead off-site seminars and will often send staff and other leaders to attend seminars. Pastors of larger churches tend to be highly selective and prefer small-group networking groups of peers or other specialists rather than large group, general-topic training events.

Megachurch pastors are sometimes criticized for their limited involvement in general meetings and conferences for pastors. Smaller church pastors often do not realize that they place large church pastors in an awkward position. When the large church pastor or staff member is asked about present affairs, he is often interpreted as boasting if he shares good news. When difficult times are shared in a private or small-group setting, this information is sometimes treated as the latest inside "confidential" gossip from an official inside source. The large church leader usually decides that it is wiser to limit the sharing of what he knows to peers of other larger churches who share similar challenges.

13. The Increasing Role of Risk

Leaders in smaller churches have the advantage of a larger awareness of the next step in growth because of an abundance of similar-size churches that make similar decisions with regularity. As a church grows larger, however, the impact of high-risk situations and the crucial nature of their success or failure tends to decrease the number of high-risk decisions.

The larger the church, the more selective and strategic is the risk-taking process. This process can be compounded when the church has a large base of innovative staff members or laymen involved in key planning roles. While innovations require time, the time between the announcement of one innovation and the need to develop the next such idea or product is relatively short. Wise leadership avoids the pressure of the "what's next?" from uninformed consumers usually found among the 34 percent who represent the "early majority." This segment of consumers usually has great need for fresh ideas but often has little appreciation for what is required to develop or receive innovative ideas.

Thankfully, all church leaders have access to the Holy Spirit, who is the source of all great ideas and is the ultimate source of innovation. Jesus reminds us, "If ye then, being evil, know how to give good gifts unto your children, how much more shall your Father which is in heaven give good things to them that ask him?" (Matt. 7:11). James, in his epistle, writes, "If any of you lack wisdom, let him ask of God, that giveth to all men liberally, and upbraideth not; and it shall be given him" (James 1:5). Finally, Paul writes, "Now unto him that is able to do exceeding abundantly above all that we ask or think, according to the power that worketh in us" (Eph. 3:20).

14. Organizational Structure

In most, but not all instances, churches grow larger by structuring small. American churches, however, tend to structure for large classes, and the result is plateaued and declining churches.

As author of the only book about the world's largest churches, this researcher discovered that the size of their groups tends to be much smaller than that of many smaller churches. The temptation of most churches is to allow groups to have an average attendance exceeding sixteen people. Most groups that are allowed to reach more than sixteen people tend to plateau, since a different set of group dynamics begins to operate at that level. Once a group reaches that many people in attendance, it tends to lose both desire and ability to reproduce.

To use David Womack's illustration, small single-cell churches tend to be structured more like a sealed-off grapefruit. Churches that grow large, however, tend to structure around new clusters of small groups like clusters of grapes. This latter model encourages the employment of a broader base of ministry among members and encourages the employment of spiritual gifts. Exceptions to this rule are usually black congregations and some Independent congregations. Both of these are organized around a strong charismatic pastor and celebrative praise worship. Success is strongly dependent on (1) the pastor retiring early enough to prevent an exodus of members, and (2) another strong pastor called by the church who shares and affirms the best qualities of the church's culture and philosophy of ministry.

15. Role of the Sunday School

Pastor and people in a small church tend to see the Sunday school's basic purpose as focused on nurture and limited attendance growth. This attendance growth, when it is allowed to happen, usually fosters "adopted" members (i.e., guests) rather than "full" members (i.e., family).

For example, shortly after I moved to Missouri, a man from that area was visiting from southern California. While waiting for our cars to be repaired, we found ourselves deep in conversation about churches and church growth. When the discussion turned to small churches, he reached into his pocket and began showing me a note pad filled with names. He explained that these names were the reason for his brief return to the region. After moving closer to show me the names, he explained that the thirteen family names on that pad were his relatives—his ancestors. The names for his ever increasing genealogy had been gathered from church cemetery tombstones, local library records, and the county courthouse.

Then, with a sense of awe, he indicated that an outsider visiting the church they all went to would probably attend for months or even years without knowing these people were all related. Outsiders, though welcomed as friends and even as welcomed guests, could never be certain whether some decisions were church decisions or family decisions. The visitor's final comment on the topic was, "Small churches have small church ways."

Meanwhile, pastors and people in growing churches have developed a sensitivity for welcoming and maturing new members and potential believers into both fullness in Christ (Eph. 3:19) and full membership (Eph. 4:11–16). This people-focus encourages both numerical growth and more effective assimilation of all members for usefulness in the life of the church (Phil. 2:9–11).

Nongrowing churches often view their Sunday schools as being primarily for children and for education. Growing churches, however, tend to see Sunday school as being for all ages and its function as reaching, teaching, evangelizing, and developing believers.

16. Growth Focus

Growth is often defined, in a smaller church, as growing larger some day in the future as the church gradually reaches new members who are basically like the present congregation. Growth is viewed as a gradual process and even as a matter of replacing faithful attenders or members who have recently moved from the area, transferred their membership to another local congregation, become inactive for various reasons, are homebound, or have recently died.

Members of growing and larger churches, however, tend to major on nurture growth while placing added attention on creating islands of ministry in the community beyond the walls of the church as the local congregation grows larger. The mere application of biblical vision generates additional energy for growth. A sense of urgency and immediacy tends to displace the tolerance for slower growth. Rapid growth is viewed as valid and at times a normal expression of growth.

17. Ecumenical Awareness

Due to limited human and strategic resources, most smaller congregations form networks of dependent cooperation for the purposes of providing ministry resources and mission initiatives. As a congregation grows, its enlarged organizational structure also tends to narrow its focus on the local ministry, rather than the network (denominational), and its own personal accountability to kingdom mandates, goals, and tasks.

18. Media Management

Avoidance and discomfort with the media, for a variety of reasons, is often a characteristic of small churches. Lack of knowledge, limited financial resources, avoidance of strangers, and satisfaction with things as they are now are common reasons why the smaller church avoids media.

The church that grows larger tends to adopt the view that the various media were created to be the servants and channels for expanded growth of the kingdom through the churches.

19. Music Ministry

Few people would question the role that music has in the growth of a congregation. While churches are growing through the use of many kinds of music, growing churches usually view music as participative and celebrative worship. In the church that remains small, the text of its music tends to be written or sung in the first and third persons. Growth churches, in contrast, are often more celebrative, with the text and the spirit of their music being written and sung in the first and second persons. The nongrowth church often sings "about" God, while the growth church frequently views congregational singing as praise "to" God.

7

Megachurches: High-Impact Ministries

Critics of megachurches regularly point out what are considered to be the problems with these largest of congregations. A man once remarked in my presence, "The Lord must love the small churches because he made so many of them." Depending on the city and region, you will find 60 to 80 percent of all United States churches to be plateaued or declining in membership and/or attendance.

Interestingly, the percentage of churches with 200 or less in attendance and that of nongrowing churches is about 80 percent of all United States churches. Are we to also assume that God intends most of his churches to be small, plateaued, and/or declining in growth? This seems highly unlikely since the Great Commission mandate of Matthew 28:19–20 has not been deleted from the Bible.

We trust that God loves all of his churches, whether they be large or small. The frequent use, however, of the commands to "go" and "grow" in the Bible strongly suggests he intends that lost sheep be found and that his churches increase in number. The issue is not small versus larger churches. The major issue remains biblical obedience, faith, and reproductive multiplication as believers. Rather than dwelling on the "problems" of megachurches, I prefer to discuss their strengths and the way these strengths can be used to reach our cities for Christ.

20 Strengths of Megachurches

1. Multiple Ministries

Cities are known for being places where there are groups of people with many varied social and cultural backgrounds. Smaller churches are usually expected to focus on ministries for people with a few specific needs or to serve as a small staff of general practitioners to several groups with many varied needs.

Large churches, like Lakewood Church of Houston, Texas, are able to provide many specialized ministries, which include the Spanish-speaking community, the hearing impaired, senior citizens, inmates in jails and prisons, seamen, the homeless, assisting missionaries in thirty-nine countries, distributing tons of gospel literature in thirty-nine countries and tens of thousands of teaching tapes into sixty-two different countries, and weekly television programs that reach into forty million homes.

Braeswood Assembly of God, also in Houston, discovered that forty-eight different countries were represented among its nearly 2,400 worshipers each week, who speak twenty-two different languages. The large migration of Hispanics into homes near the church's sanctuary led Braeswood Assembly to hire a full-time Hispanic pastor to minister to this segment of the congregation.

Allen Temple Baptist Church of Oakland, California, leads a daily apartment tutorial program with an average enrollment of 80–100 elementary- and secondary-school students. Other ministries to needy families include food programs and assistance with housing and utility bills. Through the Health Education Committee the church cooperates with Shiloh Christian Fellowship in conducting annual neighborhood health fairs that provide free health screenings by doctors, nurses, and community health agencies. The AIDS Ministry Task Force provides information, education, and help for people living with AIDS.

Numerous other megachurches—Presbyterian, Baptist, Methodist, and Independent congregations, like Capital Christian Center, Sacramento, California—provide ministries on a large scale to hurting people. This Assembly of God congregation includes under the umbrella known as "target ministries" the Bread of Life program, for men and women suffering from compulsive overeating, anorexia, or bulimia. The Pure Life/Men ministry is targeted to men who are in bondage to pornography, homosexuality, and other sexual addictions. The New Wine ministry is designed for men and women addicted to drugs and alcohol. This list, presented in miniature, reflects a much larger list of ministries offered in Jesus' name by megachurches.

2. High-Visibility Location

As a researcher who personally visits more than 200 churches annually, this writer frequently discovers almost unknown megachurches in hard-to-find places. However, many of these strategic churches eventually relocate either near or directly on major avenues and/or interstate interchanges. These easy to identify and reach locations place these churches within minutes of most of their metropolitan area. Tens of thousands of unchurched people are aware of their location.

Examples of highly visible sanctuaries include Lake Avenue Congregational Church of Pasadena, California; New Hope Community Church of Portland, Oregon; Capital Christian Center of Sacramento, California; North Phoenix Baptist Church of Phoenix, Arizona; First Baptist Church of Orlando, Florida; First Baptist Church of Houston, Texas; and Riverside Baptist Church of Denver, Colorado.

3. Specialized Staff

The structure and type of church staff varies significantly among denominational and affiliation groups. These same differences also vary as churches grow larger.

One of the best measures of these differences is shown in the *National Church Staff Salary Survey*, published every two years by the National Association of Church Business Administration.[1] This report analyzes salaries of more than twenty-five church staff positions within more than thirty denominational categories, geographically by region of the nation and by both size of annual budget and average size of Sunday-morning worship attendance.

Churches reporting average worship attendance *up to 200 people* usually have from one to eight of these more than twenty-five staff positions. While Churches of Christ, for example, tend to have only a senior minister at this size, Pentecostal churches have added one associate. Lutherans and Nazarenes tend to have three of the positions; Baptists report having four to eight of the various positions; Presbyterians have six; and Methodists report having eight of the positions in mixed assortments. The pattern varies widely among different regions of the nation. The most common salaried staff positions for churches this size include: pastor, associate, secretary, executive secretary, business administrator, minister of music, organist/pianist, minister of Christian education, youth director, maintenance person and custodian.

The churches of *201–400 worship attendance* complement the above-mentioned staff positions with administrative assistant, finance secretary, maintenance supervisor, dietician/hostess, minister of children and/or preschool, and directors for evangelism, adults, young adults, and senior adults.

At the *401–800 worship attendance* level many of the same staff positions of the churches at the 201–400 size are still employed. One major difference, however, is a much higher percentage of the 401–800 size churches reporting these salaried ministry positions.

This pattern of churches expanding the variety of ministries through additional staff is further noticed once a church's average worship attendance reaches *801–1400 people and larger*. It is common for megachurches with attendance of *2,000 or more people* to provide associates for almost every category of ministry staff.

Several have added new categories of staff, such as executive pastor (this is not the same person as the senior pastor), minister of church growth, minister of assimilation, minister of prayer, minister of media, and even research associates to assist the senior pastor in gathering specialized information for writing and sermon preparation. A senior pastor who has more than fifty staff members may have an administrative assistant and one or more secretaries responsible for his immediate office needs.

4. Name Recognition of the Church

In a city like Chicago, with at least 1,100 churches, or Boston, with nearly 400 churches, people who are active members in a church have difficulty knowing even one-fourth of churches other than their own. Unchurched people in almost any size city, even the smallest cities, are almost totally unaware of a church's name or affiliation unless it is large, is on radio or television, is known for a special ministry that interests them personally, or has a pastor well-known in the city. Megachurches are able with greater regularity and intensity to saturate a population with their names and messages through electronic and print media. They also have many more members mixing with the general population at any given time than smaller churches.

Data gathered at the Church Growth and World Missions Center at Southwest Baptist University in Missouri, for example, indicates that the churches with an average worship attendance of at least 1,000 people are consistently among the fastest-growing churches in the nation. These churches tend to saturate their cities through direct mail, door-to-door visitation, and telemarketing methods.

5. Pastor Is a Proven Leader, Preacher, and Teacher

Many new seminary graduates are surprised to learn that serving their first church, usually a small church, is different from previous expectations.

The pastor of the smaller church is expected to be a one-person staff capable of being a spiritual general practitioner. As a church grows larger and additional staff members are added, a church usually develops a larger base of leaders and begins to use long-range planning strategies.

All of these elements allow each staff member, but especially the senior pastor, to excel in leading the church to dream dreams and to reevaluate and redefine purpose and direction through well-planned teaching, preaching, and leadership. His role and abilities become increasingly clearer as that of team builder. He becomes the shepherd of his staff and key lay-leaders, who when equipped actually serve as shepherds of the congregation.

6. Many Neighborhoods Are Represented

While most smaller churches tend to represent, at most, two or three neighborhoods, megachurches are most often regional churches.

First Baptist Church of Jacksonville, Florida, for example, has a Sunday worship attendance approaching 10,000 people. The church is constructing a new 9,200-capacity worship center. Founded in the year 1846, the church currently owns eleven blocks in downtown Jacksonville. This Southern Baptist congregation decided in recent years to organize its Sunday school classes by zip-code areas.

Much like that of the Yoido Full Gospel Church of Seoul, Korea, this new structure allowed First Baptist Church to organize itself for more effective evangelistic outreach, member follow-up, and neighborhood fellowships. The church has increased in average weekly Sunday-morning worship attendance from 6,000 people in 1981–82 to 7,900 in 1991.

Second Baptist Church of Houston, Texas, has recently been listed as the fastest-growing church in North America, with an average weekly increase in worship attendance of nearly 3,000 people in a one-year period. This congregation penetrates and ministers to both members and nonmembers through regularly scheduled "zip-code fellowships."

7. Social and Community Stability

Every community constantly experiences change. People move in and people move out because of job transfers and other reasons.

Some communities are much more mobile than others. Dr. T. T. Crabtree, former pastor of First Baptist Church of Springfield, Missouri, shared that some of the children in the elementary school nearest their church site had changed schools as many as five times in one year. Because people attending megachurches come from many communities and form a unique community themselves, they are able to maintain a sense of continuity and community identity even when radical changes are taking place in the neighborhood they call home. The Germantown Baptist Church in metropolitan Memphis, Tennessee, joined other strong church groups to form a group called Urban Allies, to aid churches in radically changing communities of their city.

8. Openness to Innovative Ideas

Since megachurches are able to attract people from many geographical and special-interest communities of their cities, this invites opportunity for variety in creative resources. The great challenge of the large church is usually in finding ways to utilize creative leaders, rather than having to worry about a shortage of leaders.

The homogenous groups within a larger heterogenous congregation allow a larger forum and openness to new and bold ideas for reaching a city. Usually, the pastor and staff members of such churches have been selected by the congregation because of the success of their previous openness to ideas from others.

9. Reduced Exposure to Internal Conflict

The pastor of a small church has fewer emotional shock absorbers when conflict is encountered than can be offered by the multiple-staff church. As mentioned elsewhere in these pages, staff stability tends to increase as a church grows larger. Shared staff responsibility, adequate salaries, clear job descriptions and expectations, and opportunity to specialize in select areas of ministry reinforce the potential for greater harmony in church life.

10. Expanded Opportunity for Service

Large churches frequently offer ministry opportunity in as many as a hundred areas. Churches like Alamo City Baptist Church of San Antonio, Texas, and First Baptist Church of Springdale, Arkansas, ask new members of their congregations to complete spiritual-gift inventories. Results of the inventory are then matched with ministry opportunities available within the congregation.

Ministry opportunities are often available at almost any hour of the day or night. Volunteers are activated in the preparation of mail-outs, assisting as counselors, radio and television technical assistance, tutoring, free medical care, and multitudes of highly specialized skill areas. An example of the latter is car repair for widows and other single women.

11. Excellence of Music

Few sounds touch the heart as powerfully as that of human voices in congregational singing in churches. The mere awe of 2,000 or 10,000 Christians singing together generates a sense of conquest.

Megachurches are known in all major cities for their dynamic seasonal concerts. First Assembly of God in Phoenix, Arizona, is a pioneer in its grand Fourth of July concert; The Crystal Cathedral congregation of Garden Grove, California, is known nationally for its "flying angels" and live camels each Christmas; First Baptist Church of Orlando, Florida, has filled its 5,000-seat sanctuary with two giant singing-Christmas-tree concerts; and Second Baptist Church of Houston, Texas, is known for its legendary 400-seat choir loft and Festival of Lights each Christmas.

Orchestras composed of members of the local congregation are now a frequent sight in the largest churches. Some churches, like Eastwood Baptist Church, Marietta, Georgia, has organized both an adult and youth orchestra which serve in different worship services. Nationally known soloists who receive more invitations than they can possibly handle hesitate to accept invitations for area concerts unless they can have a guaranteed attendance. Churches with thousands in attendance each week can usually meet that need and invite smaller churches of the city to benefit from what would otherwise be an impossible dream.

12. Media Saturation of the Immediate Metropolitan Area

While radio can be expensive for most churches, television would be absolutely unthinkable. Homebound members with serious problems, multitudes who view worship services from hospital beds, aged viewers in nursing homes, prison inmates, unchurched spouses who remain home while their families attend church, and many more can be touched through electronic mass media.

13. Media Saturation into Other Cities, States, and Countries

Previously unknown churches become household names due to national radio and television exposure. When Christian families are moved by employers from one city to another almost overnight, a church in that distant city, through the media, is able to reassure a family that God's people are already present in significant strength.

Media provides for the small church pastor immediate access to his peers in much larger churches, who may nurture his own knowledge of the Scriptures. Radio and television create regional, national, and international networks of ministry that provide distinctively Christian news and other information common to the greater Christian community of churches. Government opposition to the Christian message and organized worship, immediate eye-witness coverage of social conflict involving Christians at an abortion clinic, or a Billy Graham Crusade in Hong Kong are brought directly into our homes, offices, and churches.

Many megachurches are able to broadcast by satellite directly from their sanctuaries to homes in all fifty states.

14. Organizational and Group Homogeneity

As a church grows larger, the age span between age groups becomes narrower. This allows a natural transition for flow of members from one age group to the next. Within the smaller church this alternative is not available and results in potential organizational conflict.

The large church, though by nature a very heterogenous organization, is able to provide a multitude of common interest ministry action groups. Since most megachurches are administered through delegated authority to staff and lay-leaders, it is common for a megachurch pastor to be unable to name all the ministries active within his congregation. His leaders, however, are well aware of the ministries, their health, activities, and who is involved in them. These common interest groupings are the nerve center for reproductive organizational life of the various ministries of the large church.

15. Kingdom Focus Versus Dominance by Local Culture

Most churches are able to reach beyond their local communities with the gospel through cooperative efforts with other churches. Few, however, are able to penetrate distant communities, cities, and nations with their own human and financial resources alone. This limitation of resources tends to keep the local congregation bound by the culture of its own members and community. This is both a strength and limitation.

A megachurch with significant resources meanwhile, is able to function more effectively than many smaller denominations (even though these churches may be large contributors to their own denominations, they may be perceived as a threat to the denomination). Mere awareness of this capability allows most megachurches to develop and

employ a worldview that allows penetration of the immediate community while also sharpening kingdom focus for
evangelizing entire cities. These cities may include their
own and others.

Second Baptist Church of Houston, Texas, has single-
handedly initiated the establishment of more than 90 large
Baptist congregations in Latin America. This has been accomplished while also being a regular contributor to the
Foreign Mission Board of the Southern Baptist Convention. Other megachurches can share similar accounts.

16. Financial Resources

Contrary to popular opinion, many megachurches are
not wealthy. Also contrary to general opinion, many
megachurches do not maintain huge bank reserves. Ad-
mittedly, there are exceptions.

Per capita income even for megachurches can average as
little as fifteen dollars. First Baptist Church of Hammond,
Indiana, is the largest Christian congregation in the nation.
The church averages an attendance of approximately 20,000
people each week. Vast amounts of human and financial resources are spent annually to reach the greater-Chicago population for Jesus Christ. Funds usually are expended as
quickly as they are received. This practice is considered by
the church to be a matter of good stewardship.

Large churches, however, are full of people who can re-
member small church conflicts resulting from bank-account
reserves remaining untouched for several years and in some
cases for decades. Many small churches, however, also know
the principle of allowing God to give through you as well as
to you.

17. Potential for Influencing Change in Cities

While major newspapers continue to report zoning conflicts between rapidly growing churches and municipal zon-

ing boards, megachurches remain powerful agents for social and moral change. When one major city in the Southwest attempted through parking restrictions to curb the growth of ethnic storefront churches, the megachurches of that city were able to offer vocal and legal support to the smaller congregations.

City governments have few organizations that share the concerns of the city leaders and who are able to mobilize an army of supporters to oppose drug-related crimes, abortion, poverty, joblessness, marital and family problems, racial unrest, and even community apathy. When megachurch pastors and their congregations speak about community problems, they are seldom ignored. Make no mistake, megachurches serve a key role in encouraging all churches within a city to be alert and bold in sharing the living Christ with the hurting and broken people of the city and its ever-changing communities.

18. Major Interpreters of Urban Spiritual Warfare

Neighborhood gang members in Kansas City, Brooklyn, Los Angeles, Chicago, Houston, and Miami are aware of the spiritual leaders in their communities. Power groups usually know that it is best to keep a respectable distance from worship centers, where the power of God is obviously present. These groups within a community know that pain and death are real. They know enough about hell on earth that it seems reasonable to assume the reality of an eternal hell as just payment for those they oppose in the streets.

Even nonbelievers expect Christians to be the voices for God in opposition to the darkness in the city. Christians are awakened even when a mosque or synagogue is burned or damaged by acts of violence. The enemies of the churches act foolishly when they act recklessly against God's people. Megachurches care for the welfare and health of smaller churches far more than these churches may ever know.

19. Strong Centers of Support for Christian Values

Churches of all types and sizes are regularly ignored and/or mocked by major news media. Interestingly, the same treatment is seldom directed toward groups from other religions. In a culture when the church can be its own worst enemy, due to low esteem and lack of trust of one another, we must be continually reminded that our mandate is to be the light of the world and the salt of the earth. While our culture offers success and comfort, it is also capable of robbing the churches of vitality and urgency of mission.

The Anglo, Hispanic, and black population of Houston, Texas, is reproduced in the membership of Lakewood Church. The motto of the church, Oasis of Love, can be found on the church's printed materials and over all entrances to the sanctuary. In the same way, the church is meant to be the center where unchurched non-Christian strangers, friends, and relatives can attend and bring those they love with a sure awareness that God still heals broken hearts, broken hopes, and broken homes today. The power of the changed life through Jesus Christ is central to most megachurches, which reaffirm the Bible through the pulpit, Bible classes, seminars, concerts, media evangelism, Christian schools, and a host of other ministries that affirm Christian values.

20. Umbrella for Weak Churches Ready to Disband

One of the greatest challenges for megachurches in the next generation will be learning how to strengthen weaker churches in urban centers without attracting their strongest leaders. Three churches that have excelled in meeting this need during the last half of the twentieth century have been Highland Park Baptist Church of Chattanooga, Tennessee, First Baptist Church of Dallas, Texas, and First Baptist Church of Houston, Texas. The Dallas congregation, for example, maintains a network of nearly thirty satellite chapels through which most of its benevolence resources are shared with the inner city. For almost a century this church has had almost a third of its congregation ministering through satellite locations. First Baptist Church of Houston maintains a helping relationship to more than thirty struggling churches of inner-city Houston. Megachurches are uniquely able to provide resources that are usually in decline in urban centers of the nation.

Appendix A

Directory of Affiliation Abbreviations

ABC	American Baptist Churches
AG	Assemblies of God
AME	African Methodist Episcopal
BIB	Bible Church
BGC	Baptist General Conference
CALC	Calvary Chapels
CC	Churches of Christ
CC-B	Churches of Christ-Boston
CCCC	Conservative Congregational Christian Conference
CMA	Christian and Missionary Alliance
COGC	Church of God (Cleveland)
COGIC	Church of God in Christ
DIS	Disciples of Christ
ECOV	Evangelical Covenant
EFC	Evangelical Free Church
ELCA	Evangelical Lutheran Church in America
EP	Evangelical Presbyterian
FSQ	Foursquare Gospel

IB	Independent Baptist
ICC	Independent Christian Churches
IND	Independent (non-charismatic)
INDC	Independent Charismatic
KPCA	Korean Presbyterian Church in America
L-MO	Lutheran Church-Missouri Synod
NAZ	Church of the Nazarene
NBC	National Baptist Convention
NBCA	National Baptist Convention of America
NBC/USA	National Baptist Convention, U.S.A.
PCA	Presbyterian Church of America
PCUSA	Presbyterian Church of the United States
PHC	Pentecostal Holiness Church
PNBC	Progressive National Baptist Convention
RCA	Reformed Church in America
SBC	Southern Baptist Convention
UCC	United Church of Christ
UMC	United Methodist Church
UP	United Pentecostal
WES	Wesleyan

Appendix B

U.S. Megachurches, 1990, Location by Region

West
90

Midwest
55

Northeast
22

Southeast
143

Appendix C

Fastest-Growing Churches in the U.S., 1989-90

	90–91 Gain	'90 Wor.	'91 Wor.	Church	City, State	Affiliation	Pastor
1	2000	4000	6000	New Birth M. Baptist Church	Decatur, Ga.	ABC	Eddie L. Long
	2000	8000	10000	Grace Community Church	Sun Valley, Calif.	IND	John F. MacArthur, Jr.
2	1900	4800	6700	World Changers	College Park, Calif.	INDC	Creflo Dollar
3	1850	5550	7400	Calvary Chapel	Diamond Bar, Calif	CALC	Rual Ries
4	1759	7123	8882	Calvary Church	Santa Ana, Calif.	IND**	David Hocking
5	1606	13040	14646	Willow Creek Community Church	S. Barrington, Ill.	IND	Bill Hybels
6	1600	3200	4800	Hickory Grove Baptist Church	Charlotte, N.C.	SBC	Joe B. Brown
7	1500	1800	3300	Calvary Chapel of Philadelphia	Philadelphia, Penn.	CALC	Joe Focht
	1500	4500	6000	Crossroads Cathedral	Oklahoma City, Okla.	AG	Daniel T. Sheaffer
	1500	4500	6000	Church of the Open Door	Crystal, Minn.	CMA	David Johnson
	1500	1800	3300	Ben Hill U. Methodist Church	Atlanta, Ga.	UMC	Walter L. Kimbrough**
	1500	2100	3600	Heritage Christian Center	Denver, Colo.	INDC	Dennis Leonard
8	1350	850	2200	Jesus People Ministries	Miami, Fla.	INDC	Isaiah Williams
9	1300	5700	7000	Calvary Chapel	Albuquerque, N.M.	CALC	Skip Heitzig
10	1250	12000	13250	Calvary Chapel of Costa Mesa	Santa Ana, Calif.	CALC	Chuck Smith
11	1100	1100	2200	Calvary Chapel of Ft. Lauderdale	Pompano Beach, Fla.	CALC	Robert Coy
	1100	1000	2100	Acts Full Gospel Church	Oakland, Calif.	INDC	Bob Jackson
12	1000	5000	6000	Brentwood Baptist Church	Houston, Tex.	SBC	Joe S. Ratliff
	1000	8000	9000	Harvest Christian Fellowship	Riverside, Calif.	CALC	Greg Laurie
	1000	5000	6000	South Coast Community Church	Newport Beach, Calif.	IND	Bob Shanks
	1000	7500	8500	W. Angeles Church of God in Christ	Los Angeles, Calif.	COGIC	Charles E. Blake

						COGIC	T. L. Lowery
13	952	3500	4452	Washington National Church of God	Washington, D.C.		
14	951	470	1421	Northland Community Church	Longwood, Fla.	IND	Joel C. Hunter
15	910	8476	9386	Second Baptist Church	Houston, Tex.	SBC	H. Edwin Young
16	811	3823	4634	Saddleback Valley Community Church	Mission Viejo, Calif.	SBC	Rick Warren
17	808	5666	6474	Southeast Christian Church	Louisville, Ky.	ICC	Robert L. Russell
18	800	2800	3600	Hyde Park Baptist Church	Austin, Tex.	SBC	Ralph M. Smith
19	760	2290	3050	Trinity Fellowship	Amarillo, Tex.	INDC	Jimmy Evans
20	750	1750	2500	Little Country Church	Palo Cedro, Calif.	CALC	Bryan Blank
21	725	1460	2185	Grace Korean Church	Norwalk, Calif.	KPCA	Kwang Shin Kim
22	700*	3100*	3800*	World Agape Mission Church	Los Angeles, Calif.	PHC	John Kim
23	678	5645	6323	The Chapel	Akron, Ohio	IND	Knute Larson
24	659	1622	2281	Olive Baptist Church	Pensacola, Fla.	SBC	Ted Traylor
25	650	450	1100	Assembly of God Tabernacle	Decatur, Ga.	AG	Coy R. Barker
26	635	1290	1925	Dauphin Way Baptist Church	Mobile, Ala.	SBC	Larry L. Thompson
27	626	1674	2300	Los Angeles Church of Christ	Los Angeles, Calif.	CC-B	Kip McKean & Marty Fuqua
28	600	3000	3600	Emmanuel Faith Community Church	Escondido, Calif.	IND	Richard Strauss
29	598	3250	3848	Trinity Church	Lubbock, Tex.	INDC	Randall Ross
30	593	2354	2947	Hoffmantown Baptist Church	Albuquerque, N.M.	SBC	Charles S. Lowery
31	577	1028	1605	Westside Foursquare Church	Bend, Ore.	FSQ	Ken Johnson
32	555	4050	4605	Victory Christian Center	Tulsa, Okla.	INDC	Billy Joe Daugherty

#				Church	Location		Pastor
33	552	950	1502	Custer Road United Methodist Church	Plano, Tex.	UMC	W. Mark Craig
34	543	10000	10543	First Assembly of God	Phoenix, Ariz.	AG	Tommy J. Barnett
35	521	3879	4400	Eastside Foursquare Church	Kirkland, Wash.	FSQ	Doug Murren
36	505	3875	4380	Windsor Village U. Methodist Church	Houston, Tex.	UMC	Kirbyjon H. Caldwell
37	505	1960	2465	Christ Church	Nashville, Tenn.	INDC	L. H. Hardwick, Jr.
	500	2800	3300	Riverbend Baptist Church	Austin, Tex.	SBC	Gerald Mann
	500	3500	4000	Applegate Christian Fellowship	Jacksonville, Ore.	CALC	Jon Courson
	500	600	1100	Evergreen Community Church	Burnsville, Minn.	IND	Brent Knox & Mark Parling
	500	2400	2900	Trinity United Church of Christ	Chicago, Ill.	UCC	Jeremiah Wright, Jr.
	500	1175	1675	Atlanta Church of Christ	Marietta, Ga.	CC-B	Steve Sapp
	500	2800	3300	New Life Church	Colorado Springs, Colo.	INDC	Ted Haggard
	500	3500	4000	Templo Calvario Assembly	Santa Ana, Calif.	AG	Daniel de Leon
	500	6000	6500	Crenshaw Christian Center	Los Angeles, Calif.	INDC	Fred K. C. Price
38	485	15	500	Inland Hills Church	Chino Hills, Calif.	AG	David F. Stoecklein
39	475	1425	1900	South Valley Christian Church	San Jose, Calif.	ICC	David Sawkins
40	469	2903	3372	Calvary Assembly of God	Winter Park, Fla.	AG	Mark Rutland
41	456	1286	1742	Central Christian Church	Las Vegas, Nev.	ICC	Gene Appel
42	450	1300	1750	Bethel Assembly of God	Redding, Calif.	AG	Raymond E. Larson, Jr.
43	440	305	745	Cascade Hills Baptist Church	Columbus, Ga.	SBC	Bill Purvis
44	435	815	1250	Cornerstone Assembly of God	Fresno, Calif.	AG	Terry L. Bates
45	401	2314	2715	Central Church of God	Charlotte, N.C.	COGC	H. Loran Livingston

46	400	2200	2600	Oak Cliff Bible Fellowship Church	Dallas, Tex.	BIB	Anthony Evans
	400	2600	3000	Victory Love Fellowship	Albuquerque, N.M.	IND	Robert W. Carman
	400	800	1200	Salem Baptist Church	Chicago, Ill.	IB	James T. Meeks
47	400	1800	2200	Calvary Baptist Temple	Savannah, Ga.	SBC	Len B. Turner
	400	4600	5000	Crossroads Church of Denver	Wheat Ridge, Colo.	INDC	Tom Stipe
	400	1600	2000	Faith Community Church	Covina, Calif.	INDC	James H. Reeve
	392	1338	1730	Indiana Ave. Baptist Church	Lubbock, Tex.	SBC	Jon D. Randles
48	390	1675	2065	First Baptist North Spartanburg	N. Spartanburg, S.C.	SBC	Mike Hamlet
	390	1110	1500	Assembly of God	Covina, Calif.	AG	Ronald E. Stevens
49	374	1376	1750	Glide Memorial U. Memorial Church	San Francisco, Calif.	UMC	Cecil Williams
50	363	400	763	Fellowship of Los Colinas	Irving, Tex.	SBC	Ed Young, Jr.
51	352	2358	2710	Chicago Church of Christ	Berkeley, Ill.	CC-B	Ron Drabot
	352	2027	2379	Johnson Ferry Baptist Church	Marietta, Ga.	SBC	G. Bryant Wright
52	350	1250	1600	Christ Community Church	Franklin, Tenn.	PCA	Scottie Smith
	350	900	1250	Resurrection Life Full Gospel Church	Grandville, Mich.	INDC	Duane Vander Klok
	350	900	1250	Centenary United Methodist Church	Lexington, Ky.	UMC	Alfred W. Gwinn, Jr.
53	347	753	1100	Life Center	Spokane, Wash.	FSQ	Joe Wittwer
54	345	375	720	Faith Baptist Church	Victorville, Calif.	SBC	Ron Hogue
55	343	2683	3026	Sagemont Baptist Church	Houston, Tex.	SBC	John Morgan
56	342	1808	2150	Big Valley Grace Community Church	Modesto, Calif.	IND	David Seifert

57	338	1120	1458	King of Kings Lutheran Church	Omaha, Neb.	L-MO	Bradley D. Hoefs
58	330	2435	2765	College Avenue Baptist Church	San Diego, Calif.	BGC	Gerald Sheveland
59	312	1833	2145	Two Rivers Baptist Church	Nashville, Tenn.	SBC	Jerry Sutton
60	308	1407	1715	First Baptist Church	Woodstock, Ga.	SBC	Johnny Hunt
61	305	375	680	Evangel Temple Assembly of God	Gahanna, Ohio	AG	Eugene D. Speich
	305	2718	3023	Southland Christian Church	Lexington, Ky.	ICC	Wayne B. Smith
62	300	6000	6300	Elmbrook Church	Waukesha, Wis.	IND	Stuart Briscoe
	300	3000	3300	Crossroads Community Church	Vancouver, Wash.	CALC	Bill Ritchie
	300	2700	3000	Alamo City Baptist Church	San Antonio, Tex.	SBC	David C. Walker
	300	3500	3800	Champion Forest Baptist Church	Houston, Tex.	SBC	O. Damon Shook
	300	2100	2400	Metropolitan Baptist Church	Houston, Tex.	SBC	Curt Dodd
	300	700	1000	Central Baptist Church	Oak Ridge, Tenn.	SBC	Ron Herrod
	300	500	800	Redeemer Presbyterian Church	New York, N.Y.	PCUSA	Timothy J. Keller
	300	1500	1800	Evangel Church	Upper Marlboro, Md.	INDC	Don D. Meares
	300	700	1000	Christ Community Church	St. Charles, Ill.	IND	Jim Nicodem
	300	50	350	Metro Heights Baptist Church	Stockbridge, Ga.	SBC	Calvin Yarbrough
	300	2200	2500	First Baptist Church	Snellville, Ga.	SBC	James Merritt
	300	4300	4600	First Baptist Church	Orlando, Fla.	SBC	Jim Henry
	300	1200	1500	First Baptist Church	Leesburg, Fla.	SBC	Charles Roesel
	300	1400	1700	First Presbyterian Church	Ft. Lauderdale, Fla.	PCUSA	Richard M. Cromie

* Includes missions.
** Pastor now serves another congregation.
1991 UMC attendance will be available in the 1992 General Minutes to be released later in 1993.

Appendix D

Largest Churches in the U.S., 1990 Worship Attendance

Worship Attendance	Church	City, State	Affiliation	Pastor
20000	First Baptist Church†	Hammond, Ind.	IB	Jack Hyles
13003	Willow Creek Community Church‡	South Barrington, Ill.	IND	Bill Hybels
12000	Calvary Chapel	Santa Ana, Calif.	CALC	Chuck Smith
10543	First Assembly of God	Phoenix, Ariz.	AG	Tommy J. Barnett
9175	Mount Paran Church of God	Atlanta, Ga.	COGC	Paul Walker
8476	Second Baptist Church	Houston, Tex.	SBC	H. Edwin Young
8250	Calvary Chapel	Downy, Calif.	CALC	Jeff Johnson
8212	Deliverance Evangelistic Church	Philadelphia, Pa.	INDC	Benjamin Smith
8000	Grace Community Church	Sun Valley, Calif.	BIB	John MacArthur
8000	Harvest Fellowship	Riverside, Calif.	CALC	Greg Laurie
7800	First Baptist Church	Jacksonville, Fla.	SBC	H. Lindsey Jr./Jerry Vines
7625	First Baptist Church	Dallas, Tex.	SBC	W. A. Criswell*
7500	West Angeles Church of God	Los Angeles, Calif.	COGIC	Charles E. Blake
7400	Chapel Hill Harvester	Decatur, Ga.	INDC	Earl Paulk
7123	Calvary Church	Santa Ana, Calif.	IND	David Hocking*
7001	Bellevue Baptist Church	Cordova, Tenn.	SBC	Adrian Rogers
7000	Lakewood Church	Houston, Tex.	INDC	John Osteen
6621	Crystal Cathedral	Garden Grove, Calif.	RCA	Robert H. Schuller
6500	Pleasant Grove M. Baptist Church	Houston, Tex.	NBC/USA	Charles Jackson
6200	Overlake Christian Church	Kirkland, Wash.	ICC	Bob Moorehead
6150	First Baptist Church	Houston, Tex.	SBC	John Bisagno
6000	Elmbrook Church	Waukesha, Wis.	IND	Stuart Briscoe
6000	Beaverton Foursquare Church	Beaverton, Ore.	FSQ	Ron Mehl

6000	Crenshaw Christian Center	Los Angeles, Calif.	INDC	Fred K. C. Price
6000	Calvary Chapel	W. Covina, Calif.	CALC	Raul Ries
5900	Capital Christian Center	Sacramento, Calif.	AG	Glen D. Cole
5800	New Hope Community Church	Portland, Ore.	INDC	Dale E. Galloway
5800	Peachtree Presbyterian Church	Atlanta, Ga.	PCUSA	Frank Harrington
5787	Mount Olivet Lutheran Church	Minneapolis, Minn.	ELCA	Paul M. Youngdahl
5700	Calvary Chapel	Albuquerque, N.M.	CALC	Skip Heitzig
5666	Southeast Christian Church	Louisville, Ky.	ICC	Robert L. Russell
5645	Chapel in University Park	Akron, Ohio	IND	Knute Larson
5500	Horizon Fellowship	San Diego, Calif.	CALC	Mike McIntosh
5345	Church on the Way	Van Nuys, Calif.	FSQ	Jack Hayford
5210	Full Gospel Tabernacle	Orchard Park, N.Y.	AG	Tommy Reid
5200	Trinity Baptist Church	San Antonio, Tex.	SBC	Buckner Fanning
5160	Young Nak Presbyterian Church	Los Angeles, Calif.	KPCA	Hee Min Park
5048	Oriental Mission Church	Los Angeles, Calif.	IND	Byung H. Lee
5000	Brentwood Baptist Church	Houston, Tex.	SBC	Joe S. Ratliff
5000	Bethany World Prayer Center	Baker, La.	INDC	Larry Stockstill
5000	Hartford Memorial Baptist Church	Detroit, Mich.	PNBC	Charles Adams
5000	South Coast Community Church	Newport Beach, Calif.	INDC	Bob Shank
5000	World Harvest Church	Columbus, Ohio	INDC	Rod Parsley
4800	Mount Ephraim Baptist Church	Atlanta, Ga.	NBC	R. L. White
4700	First Assembly of God	Tacoma, Wash.	AG	Fulton W. Buntain
4700	Word of Faith Center	Detroit, Mich.	INDC	Keith Butler
4680	First Baptist Church	Atlanta, Ga.	SBC	Charles Stanley
4600	Crossroads Church—Denver	Wheatridge, Colo.	INDC	Tom Stipe

4500	Roswell Street Baptist Church	Marietta, Ga.	SBC	Nelson Price
4500	People's Church	Fresno, Calif.	AG	George L. Johnson
4500	Crossroads Cathedral	Oklahoma City, Okla.	AG	Daniel T. Sheaffer
4500	Church of the Open Door	Crystal, Minn.	CMA	David Johnson
4500	Emmanuel Faith Community Church	Escondido, Calif.	IND	Richard Strauss
4452	Washington National Church of God	Fort Washington, Md.	COGC	T. L. Lowery
4400	Bethel A.M.E. Church	Baltimore, Md.	AME	Frank M. Reid III
4390	Boston Church of Christ	Woburn, Mass.	CC	Randy McKean
4300	Christian Life Center	Stockton, Calif.	UP	Kenneth F. Haney
4200	Trinity Baptist Church	Jacksonville, Fla.	IB	Bob Gray
4200	Christian Faith Center	Seattle, Wash.	IND	Casey Treat
4200	Faith Fellowship Outreach	Edison, N.J.	INDC	David DeMola
4120	First Baptist Church	Milford, Ohio	SBC	Charles Keen
4120	Prestonwood Baptist Church	Dallas, Tex.	SBC	Jack Graham
4100	First Baptist Church	Jackson, Miss.	SBC	Frank Pollard
4079	Central Church	Memphis, Tenn.	IND	James Latimer
4050	Victory Christian Center	Tulsa, Okla.	INDC	Billy Joe Daugherty
4000	Coral Ridge Presbyterian Church	Fort Lauderdale, Fla.	PCA	D. James Kennedy
4000	Sweetwater Church, Valley	Glendale, Ariz.	INDC	Glen Foster
4000	First Baptist Church	Euless, Tex.	SBC	Jimmy Draper*
3897	Cornerstone Church	San Antonio, Tex.	INDC	John C. Hagee
3883	San Jacinto Baptist Church	Amarillo, Tex.	SBC	Stan Coffey
3879	Eastside Foursquare Church	Kirkland, Wash.	FSQ	Doug Murren
3875	Windsor Village United Methodist Church	Houston, Tex.	UMC	Kirbyjon H. Caldwell

3843	First Baptist Church	Orlando, Fla.	SBC	Jim Henry
3823	Saddleback Community Church	Mission Viejo, Calif.	SBC	Rick Warren
3768	Valley Cathedral	Phoenix, Ariz.	INDC	Donald Price
3750	Faith Tabernacle	Oklahoma City, Okla.	AG	Coy R. Barker
3750	Loveland Missionary Baptist Church	Fontana, Calif.	SBC	Charles Singleton
3750	Evangel Christian Center	Louisville, Ky.	AG	Bob Rodgers
3747	First Assembly of God	Grand Rapids, Mich.	AG	Wayne M. Benson, Sr.
3679	Rolling Hills Covenant Church	Rolling Hills Estate, Calif.	ECOV	Gordon E. Kirk*
3540	First Presbyterian Church	Mt. Clemens, Mich.	PCUSA	Robert W. Battles, Jr.
3527	Frazer Memorial Methodist Church	Montgomery, Al.	UMC	John Mathison
3510	Madison Church of Christ	Madison, Tenn.	CC	Steve Flatt
3500	Full Faith Church of Love	Shawnee, Kans.	INDC	Ernie Gruen
3500	Templo Calvario	Santa Ana, Calif.	AG	Daniel de Leon
3500	Mississippi Boulevard Christian Church	Memphis, Tenn.	DIS	Alvin O. Jackson
3500	Allen Temple Baptist Church	Oakland, Calif.	ABC	J. Alfred Smith, Jr.
3500	Akron Baptist Temple	Akron, Ohio	IB	Charles Billington
3500	Xenos Christian Fellowship	Columbus, Ohio	INDC	Dennis McCallum
3500	Chapel on N. Forrest Road	Williamsville, N.Y.	INDC	James W. Andrews
3500	Concord Baptist Church	Dallas, Tex.	NBCA	E. K. Bailey
3500	Applegate Christian Center	Jacksonville, Ore.	CALC	John Courson
3400	Champion Forest Baptist Church	Houston, Tex.	SBC	O. Damon Shook
3384	Cherry Hills Community Church	Englewood, Colo.	EP	J. M. Dixon
3384	Cherry Creek Presbyterian Church	Englewood, Colo.	EP	Mark A. Brewer

3374	Scottsdale Bible Church	Scottsdale, Ariz.	IND	Darryl DelHousaye
3350	Higher Dimensions Center	Tulsa, Okla.	INDC	Carlton Pearson
3329	Menlo Park Presbyterian Church	Menlo Park, Calif.	PCUSA	Walt Gerber
3315	Lake Avenue Congregational Church	Pasadena, Calif.	CCCC	Gordon Kirk
3300	Highland Park Presbyterian	Dallas, Tex.	PCUSA	B. Clayton Bell, Sr.

Note: This listing excludes churches that prefer not to share their growth data.

★ No longer pastor at this church.

† First Baptist Church of Hammond, Indiana has not recently responded with a written update of worship attendance figures.

‡ The Willow Creek Community Church of South Barrington, Illinois, now reports the highest week-by-week worship attendance in the nation. Attendance in 1992 exceeds 14,000 each weekend at Willow Creek Community Church.

Appendix E

Largest Sunday Schools in the U.S., 1991 Attendance

Sunday School Attendance	Church	City, State	Affiliation	Pastor
20000†	First Baptist Church	Hammond, Ind.	IB	Jack Hyles
10543***	First Assembly of God	Phoenix, Ariz.	AG	Tommy J. Barnett
9336***	Metro Assembly of God	Brooklyn, N.Y.	AG	Bill Wilson
9000	Harvest Christian Fellowship	Riverside, Calif	CALC	Greg Laurie
7629	Willow Creek Community Church	South Barrington, Ill.	IND	Bill Hybels
7558***	First Baptist Church	Dallas, Tex.	SBC	Joel C. Gregory
6654	First Baptist Church	Jacksonville, Fla.	SBC	H. Lindsey Jr. / Jerry Vines
6004†	University Presbyterian Church	Seattle, Wash.	PCUSA	Earl Palmer
5583	Second Baptist Church	Houston, Tex.	SBC	H. Edwin Young
5210	Capital Christian Center	Sacramento, Calif.	AG	Glen D. Cole
5176	Bellevue Baptist Church	Cordova, Tenn.	SBC	Adrian Rogers
4820	First Baptist Church	Houston, Tex.	SBC	John Bisagno
4675	First Assembly of God	Tacoma, Wash.	AG	Fulton W. Buntain
4500†	Crossroads Cathedral	Oklahoma City, Okla.	AG	Daniel T. Sheaffer
4486	First Assembly of God	Grand Rapids, Mich.	AG	Wayne M. Benson, Sr.
4250	Trinity Baptist Church	Jacksonville, Fla.	IB	Bob Gray
4205	Prestonwood Baptist Church	Dallas, Tex.	SBC	Jack Graham
3750‡	New Life Church	Philadelphia, Pa.	AG	Tony McCreary
3700‡	Grace Community Church	Sun Valley, Calif.	BIB	John MacArthur
3601	First Baptist Church	Orlando, Fla.	SBC	Jim Henry
3500‡	Calvary Church	Santa Ana, Calif.	IND	David Hocking*
3327	First Baptist Church	Atlanta, Ga.	SBC	Charles Stanley

3190	Chapel in University Park	Akron, Ohio	Knute Larson	IND
3060	Hyde Park Baptist Church	Austin, Tex.	Ralph M. Smith	SBC
3007	First Baptist Church	Midland, Tex.	James C. Denison	SBC
3000	Skyline Wesleyan Church	Lemon Grove, Calif.	John Maxwell	WES
2900‡	Peachtree Presbyterian Church	Atlanta, Ga.	Frank Harrington	PCUSA
2896	Green Acres Baptist Church	Tyler, Tex.	David O. Dykes	SBC
2819	First Baptist Church	Arlington, Tex.	Charles R. Wade	SBC
2800†	Happy Church	Denver, Colo.	Wallace R. Hickey	AG
2794	First Baptist Church	Euless, Tex.	Jimmy Draper*	SBC
2771	Central Church	Memphis, Tenn.	James Latimer	IND
2722	Ward Evangelical Presbyterian Church	Livonia, Mich.	Bartlett L. Hess	EP
2714	Mount Paran Church of God	Atlanta, Ga.	Paul L. Walker	COGC
2684	Champion Forest Baptist Church	Houston, Tex.	O. Damon Shook	SBC
2674	Templo Calvario Assembly	Santa Ana, Calif.	Daniel de Leon	AG
2651	First Baptist Church	Springdale, Ark.	Ronnie Floyd	SBC
2588†	Grace Presbyterian Church	Peoria, Ill.	Bruce Dunn	PCUSA
2569	First Baptist Church	Jackson, Miss.	Frank Pollard	SBC
2550‡	Highland Park Presbyterian Church	Dallas, Tex.	B. Clayton Bell	PCUSA
2536	Sagemont Baptist Church	Houston, Tex.	John Morgan	SBC
2529‡	Assembly of God	Pace, Fla.	Glyn Lowery, Jr.	AG
2504‡	Southeast Christian Center	Louisville, Ky.	Robert L. Russell	ICC
2500	Young Nak Presbyterian Church	Los Angeles, Calif.	Hee Min Park	KPCA
2500	Park Cities Baptist Church	Dallas, Tex.	James L. Pleitz	SBC
2466‡	Lake Avenue Congregational Church	Pasadena, Calif.	Gordon Kirk	CCCC

2374	Saddleback Valley Community Church	Mission Viejo, Calif.	SBC	Rick Warren
2360	Madison Church of Christ	Madison, Tenn.	CC	Steve Flatt
2359	Shades Mount Baptist Church	Birmingham, Ala.	SBC	Charles Carter
2323	Graceland Baptist Church	New Albany, Ind.	SBC	Steve Marcum
2320	Lakeview Temple	Indianapolis, Ind.	AG	Thomas Paino
2316	Roswell Street Baptist Church	Marietta, Ga.	SBC	Nelson Price
2300†	Washington National Church of God	Fort Washington, Md.	COGC	T. L. Lowery
2291	Wheaton Bible Church	Wheaton, Ill.	BIB	David Krental
2263	First Southern Baptist Church	Del City, Okla.	SBC	Tom Elliff
2258	Highview Baptist Church	Louisville, Ky.	SBC	William Hancock
2255	First Baptist Church	Amarillo, Tex.	SBC	Ben Loring
2237	Casas Adobes Baptist Church	Tucson, Ariz.	SBC	Roger Barrier, Jr.
2229	Rehobeth Baptist Church	Tucker, Ga.	SBC	Richard G. Lee
2225	Grace Community Church	Tempe, Ariz.	BIB	Larry Finch
2225†	First Presbyterian Church	Flint, Mich.	PCUSA	William N. Jackson
2218	Frazer Memorial United Methodist Church	Montgomery, Ala.	UMC	John Mathison
2200	Briarwood Presbyterian Church	Birmingham, Ala.	PCUSA	Frank Barker
2183	Mount Hope Church	Lansing, Mich.	AG	David R. Williams
2170	Travis Avenue Baptist Church	Fort Worth, Tex.	SBC	Interim Pastor
2170	Trinity Baptist Church	San Antonio, Tex.	SBC	Buckner Fanning
2169	First Baptist Church	Pasadena, Tex.	SBC	Charles Redmond
2117	First Baptist Church	Jonesboro, Ga.	SBC	Charles Carter
2109	Full Gospel Tabernacle	Orchard Park, N.Y.	AG	Thomas F. Reid

2098	Hickory Grove Baptist Church	Charlotte, N.C.	SBC	Joe B. Brown
2096	People's Church	Fresno, Calif.	AG	George L. Johnson
2090	Metro Assembly of God	Cleveland, Ohio	AG	James W. Davidson
2082	Menlo Park Presbyterian Church	Menlo Park, Calif.	PCUSA	Walt Gerber
2069	Cottage Hill Baptist Church	Mobile, Ala.	SBC	Fred Wolfe
2048	Calvary Temple	Irving, Tex.	AG	J. Don George
2047	Hoffmantown Baptist Church	Albuquerque, N.M.	SBC	Charles Lowery*
2046	First Baptist Church	W. Palm Beach, Fla.	SBC	Keith Thomas
2045	Eastside Baptist Church	Marietta, Ga.	SBC	Clark Hutchinson*
2044	First Baptist Church	Roanoke, Va.	SBC	Charles Fuller
2042	First Baptist Church	Norfolk, Va.	SBC	Kenneth S. Hemphill*
2000	First Presbyterian Church	Greensboro, N.C.	PCUSA	Jerold Shetler
2000	Iglesia Puerta Del Cielo	El Paso, Tex.	AG	Marco A. Aquire
1996†	Myers Park Presbyterian Church	Charlotte, N.C.	PCUSA	Timothy Croft
1984	Calvary Baptist Church	Winston-Salem, N.C.	SBC	Mark Corts
1981	Braeswood Assembly of God	Houston, Tex.	AG	Earl J. Banning
1980	First Baptist Church	Carrollton, Tex.	SBC	Wayne Allen
1971	Whitesburg Baptist Church	Huntsville, Ala.	SBC	Jimmy E. Jackson
1960†	Trinity United Presbyterian Church	Santa Ana, Calif.	PCUSA	George Munzing
1945	Community Church of Joy	Glendale, Ariz.	ELCA	Walt P. Kallestad
1936	Dawson Memorial Baptist Church	Birmingham, Ala.	SBC	Gary Fenton
1920‡	Calvary Church	Charlotte, N.C.	IND	Ross S. Rhoads
1900‡	Los Gatos Christian Church	Los Gatos, Calif.	ICC	Daniel Henderson
1900‡	First Presbyterian Church	Jackson, Miss.	PCUSA	James Baird
1886	Germantown Baptist Church	Germantown, Tenn.	SBC	Ken Story

1870†	Coral Ridge Presbyterian Church	Ft. Lauderdale, Fla.	PCA	D. James Kennedy
1840	Trinity Life Center	Las Vegas, Nev.	AG	Richard M. Guerra
1832	First Baptist Church	Lubbock, Tex.	SBC	Hayes Wicker
1824	Eastwood Baptist Church	Tulsa, Okla.	SBC	Ruffin Snow
1815	First Church of the Nazarene	Bethany, Okla.	NAZ	Melvin McCullough
1800	First Presbyterian Church	Colorado Springs, Colo.	PCUSA	John H. Stevens
1800‡	First Presbyterian Church	Orlando, Fla.	PCUSA	J. Howard Edington
1800	Metro Assembly of God	Atlanta, Ga.	AG	Karen D. Bennett
1800†	Grace Presbyterian Church	Houston, Tex.	PCUSA	David G. McKechnie

Note: This listing excludes churches that prefer not to share their growth data.

* No longer pastor at this church.

† 1990 attendance confirmed in writing by First Baptist Church, Hammond, Ind.

‡ 1990 attendance.

*** Includes satellite worship.

Address: 1202 E. Austin, Bolivar, MO 65613, USA.
Telephone (417) 326-1773, FAX (417) 326-1783.
Correspondence welcome.

Notes

Introduction

1. Richard Jackson, "It's on My Heart," *The Word*, June 8, 1983.
2. John N. Vaughan, *The World's 20 Largest Churches* (Grand Rapids: Baker, 1984), 158.
3. "Global Glimpses," *The Commission*, October–November 1990, 4, 64.
4. John N. Vaughan, *The Large Church: A Twentieth-Century Expression of the First Century Church* (Grand Rapids: Baker, 1985).

Chapter 1

1. David Yonggi Cho, *Answers to Your Questions* (Seoul: Church Growth International, 1984), 35.
2. John N. Vaughan, *The World's 20 Largest Churches* (Grand Rapids: Baker, 1984).
3. C. Peter Wagner, *Look Out! The Pentecostals Are Coming* (Carol Stream, Ill.: Creation House, 1973).
4. C. Peter Wagner, *Stop the World, I Want to Get On* (Glendale, Calif.: Regal, 1974).
5. William R. Read, *New Patterns of Church Growth in Brazil* (Grand Rapids: Eerdmans, 1965).
6. Christian Lalive d'Epinay, *Haven of the Masses: A Study of the Pentecostal Movement in Chile* (London: Lutterworth, 1969).
7. Elmer L. Towns, *The Ten Largest Sunday Schools and What Makes Them Grow* (Grand Rapids: Baker, 1969).
8. Ibid., 154–55.
9. Elmer L. Towns, *The World's Largest Sunday School* (Nashville: Nelson, 1974).
10. Lee Lebsack, *Ten at the Top: How 10 of America's Largest Assemblies of God Grew* (Stow, Ohio: New Hope Press, 1974).
11. Eugene Skelton, *10 Fastest Growing Southern Baptist Sunday Schools* (Nashville: Convention Press, 1974).
12. Staff of *Decision* magazine, *Great Churches of Today* (Minneapolis: World Wide Publications, 1973).

13. Elmer L. Towns, John N. Vaughan, and David J. Seifert, *The Complete Book of Church Growth* (Wheaton: Tyndale, 1981).

14. Sid Smith, *10 Super Sunday Schools in the Black Community* (Nashville: Broadman, 1986).

15. *Church Growth Today*, Dr. John N. Vaughan, editor, is published six times annually. 1202 E. Austin, Bolivar, MO 65613.

16. John N. Vaughan, "North America's Fastest Growing Churches 1988–1989: Black Churches Dominate List of Ten Fastest Growing Churches," *Church Growth Today*, November–December 1990, 1.

17. Ibid., 2.

18. Thomas F. Mathews, *The Early Churches of Constantinople: Architecture and Liturgy* (University Park, Pa.: Pennsylvania State University Press, 1971).

19. John N. Vaughan, *The Large Church: A Twentieth-Century Expression of the First-Century Church* (Grand Rapids: Baker, 1985), 43–44.

20. Ed Reese, *Christian Hall of Fame Series,* vols. 1–39 (Glenwood, Ill.: Fundamental Publishers, 1975, 1976).

21. Carter G. Woodson, *The History of the Black Church*, 3rd ed. (Washington, D.C.: The Associated Publishers, 1972), 254.

22. Francis M. Arant, *"P.H."—the Welshimer Story* (Cincinnati: Standard, 1958), 46–47.

23. Vaughan, *The Large Church*, 39–64.

24. Louis Entzminger, *How to Organize and Administer a Great Sunday School* (Fort Worth: The Manney Company, 1949), iii.

Chapter 2

1. Sherri Brown, "The Search for Saddleback Sam," *MissionsUSA* (July/August 1988), 13.

2. John N. Vaughan, "North America's Fastest Growing Churches 1988–1989," *Church Growth Today*, November–December 1990, 2.

3. C. Peter Wagner, "Church Growth," in Stanley M. Burgess and Gary B. McGee, eds., *Dictionary of Pentecostal and Charismatic Movements,* (Grand Rapids: Baker, 1988), 187.

4. Carl F. George, *Prepare Your Church for the Future* (Tarrytown, N.Y.: Revell, 1991), 51.

5. Ibid., 51–52.

6. Ibid., 54.

7. Ibid., 50.

8. Peter F. Drucker, *The New Realities* (New York: Harper & Row, 1989), 200.

9. Peter F. Drucker, *Managing for the Future* (New York: Dutton, 1992), 255.

10. John N. Vaughan, *The World's 20 Largest Churches* (Grand Rapids: Baker, 1984), 25–33.

11. John N. Vaughan, *The Large Church: A Twentieth Century Expression of the First Century Church* (Grand Rapids: Baker, 1985), 39–64.

12. Edith Draper, ed., *The Almanac of the Christian World: 1991–1992* (Wheaton: Tyndale, 1990), 361–68.

13. Jerry Falwell and Elmer Towns, *Church Aflame* (Nashville: Impact Books, 1971), 190.

14. Ibid., 81.

15. C. Peter Wagner, *Leading Your Church to Growth* (Ventura: Regal, 1984), 17–18.

Chapter 3

1. John N. Vaughan, *The World's 20 Largest Churches* (Grand Rapids, Baker, 1984), 37.

2. Ibid., 36.

3. Lawrence O. Richards, *A New Face for the Church* (Grand Rapids: Zondervan, 1970), 24.

4. Lyle E. Schaller, *Looking in the Mirror* (Nashville: Abingdon, 1984), 16, 32–37.

5. C. Peter Wagner, "Church Growth," in Stanley M. Burgess and Gary B. McGee, eds., *Dictionary of Pentecostal and Charismatic Movements* (Grand Rapids: Baker, 1988), 187.

6. Elmer L. Towns, John N. Vaughan, and David J. Seifert, *The Complete Book of Church Growth* (Wheaton: Tyndale, 1981), 103.

7. C. Peter Wagner in the *Dictionary of Pentecostal and Charismatic Movements*, page 187, mentions that only two Brazilian megachurches were included in the book and that eight Assemblies of God were omitted from the list. Actually, ten rather than eight were listed on page 260 of *The World's 20 Largest Churches* and a clear explanation for their exclusion from the general listing was given on pages 19–20. Any listing of megachurch/metachurch growth rates becomes outdated annually because of dramatic growth occurring in this domain.

8. Louis Entzminger, *How to Organize and Administer a Great Sunday School* (Fort Worth: The Manney Company, 1949), 56–57.

9. Ibid., iii.

10. J. N. Barnette, *The Pull of the People* (Nashville: Convention Press, 1956), 38.

Chapter 4

1. Paul C. Glick, "Family Trends in the United States, 1890 to 1940," *American Sociological Review*, August 1942, 505.

2. Ibid., 510.

3. R. J. Johnston, *The American Urban System* (New York: St. Martin's Press, 1982), 320.

4. David A. Heenan, *The New Corporate Frontier: The Big Move to Small Town, U.S.A.* (New York: McGraw-Hill, 1991), 38.

5. Ibid., 38.

6. Ibid., 4.

7. Ibid., 6.

8. John Naisbitt and Patricia Aburdene, *Megatrends 2000: Ten Directions for the 1990's* (New York: William Morrow, 1990), 305–6.

9. Heenan, *New Corporate Frontier*, 30–31.

10. Joel Garreau, *Edge City: Life on the New Frontier* (New York: Doubleday, 1991).

11. Joel Garreau, "Edge City: Life on the New Frontier," *American Demographics*, September 1991, 24.

12. Joel Garreau, *Edge City*, 30.

13. Ibid., 26.

14. Ibid., 53.

15. Ibid., 31.

16. Jerome P. Cavanaugh, "The Urban Crisis—An Analysis," in *The Urban Crisis*, ed. David McKenna (Grand Rapids: Zondervan, 1969), 12.

17. Ibid., 13.

18. Ibid.

19. Ibid.

20. U. S. Department of Commerce, *State and Metropolitan Area Data Book 1991, 4th ed.* (Washington, D.C.: Government Printing Office, 1991), 355.

21. Ibid., 353.

22. Brad Edmondson, "Census Reveals 33 New Urban Markets," *American Demographics*, November 1991, 8.

23. Joe Schwartz and Thomas Exter, "This World Is Flat," *American Demographics*, April 1991, 36.

24. Ibid., 34.

25. Hans Blumenfeld, *The Modern Metropolis: Its Origins, Growth, Characteristics, and Planning* (Cambridge, Mass.: M.I.T. Press, 1967), 67.

26. *Information Please Almanac Atlas & Yearbook 1992*, 45th ed. (Boston: Houghton Mifflin Company, 1992), 773–83.

27. *Almanac Atlas*, 180-200.

Chapter 5

1. Warren J. Hartman and Robert L. Wilson, *The Large Membership Church* (Nashville: Discipleship Resources, 1989), 2.

2. Ibid., 3.

3. John N. Vaughan, "America's 500 Fastest Growing Churches: Part 2 of 5," *Church Growth Today*, vol. 2, no. 5, 1987, 2.

Chapter 6

1. Chuck Smith and Hugh Steven, *The Reproducers* (Glendale, Calif.: Regal, 1972), 21.

2. John N. Vaughan, *The World's 20 Largest Churches* (Grand Rapids: Baker, 1984), 194.

3. Sarah Zimmerman, "Want High Baptism Rates? Use Traditional Methods," *The Baptist Messenger* (Oklahoma), January 16, 1992, 15.

4. Chip Alford, "Pastor, Church Must Overcome Barriers for Long Tenure," *Facts & Trends*, March 1992, 8.

5. Everett M. Rogers, *Diffusion of Innovations*, 3rd ed. (New York: The Free Press, 1983), 247–51.

Chapter 7

1. Michael J. Springer and Marvin Meyer, *1992 National Church Staff Salary Survey* (Fort Worth: National Association of Church Business Administration: 1992).

Index

141